FILTERED IMAGES

WOMEN REMEMBERING THEIR GRANDMOTHERS

Edited by

SUSAN L. AGLIETTI

Orinda, California
1992

Library of Congress Catalog Card Number
91-66128

ISBN 0-9614375-1-0

Printed in the United States of America
by McNaughton & Gunn, Inc.

Cover Design and Layout by Marilyn C. Hajjar
Orinda, California

Typesetting by Comp-Type, Inc.
Fort Bragg, California

DEDICATION

On a personal level, this book is dedicated to the memory of my paternal grandmother, Bess Enda Burke, who could always find room for one more at the Seder table. It is also dedicated to the memory of my father, Gerald Burke, who nurtured my career in publishing and provided the link to my grandmother.

Additionally, FILTERED IMAGES has been compiled as a tribute to the individual grandmothers each contributor remembers and, in a larger sense, to grandmothers everywhere.

CONTENTS

WAITING FOR THEM TO SPEAK
A Portrait / A Collage, *Marian Olson* 9
Grandmother I Never Knew, *Elaine Starkman* 11
The Photograph, *Dee Burnlees* 12
Debt, *Sharon Parten Gaskill* 13
Portraits: Foremothers, *Jane Hill Purtle* 15
Grandmother's Eyes, *Ingrid Reti* 19
Sepia Tone, *Rosalie MacCary* 20
The Lizards and the Worms, *Nancy Kay Webb* 21
To Those I Never Knew, *Janet Overmyer* 26

BORDERS OF TIME
Grandma Merta and Me, *Joyce McMillin Everett* 31
Cameo, *Delores Goodrick Beggs* 32
Lillian, *Lynn Buck* 33
The Tender Heart, *Alice E. Sink* 34
Bryna Bas Yosef Halevi, *Shulamith Surnamer* 38
Going to Bed After Eight, *Lynette Seator* 39
Quiet Rooms, Empty Places, *Betty Anholt* 40
Quiet Time, *Deloris Selinsky* 44
Something to Hold, *Donna D. Vitucci* 45
Portrait of Elvira, *Lynn Buck* 51
Two Women, *Rhoda Gersten* 53
Nana, *Pamela Powell* 55
The Braid, *Cheryl Marie Wade* 60
I Knew My Grandma, *Mary Sewall-Hebert* 61
Over the River and Through the Woods, *Nancy Mathews* 62
A Cautionary Tale, *Carol Biederman* 64
Bittersweet, *Mary M. Harris* 66
Paper White Faces, *Judith Strickert Montoya* 67

A FRACTION OF HER GOODNESS
Life Lines, *Arline G. Cogan* 73
Dreams of You, *Gayle Hunter Sheller* 74
The Legacy, *Cos Barnes* 76
The Buddha, *June Hudson* 79
The Changing Embrace, *Colleen J. Houghtaling* 80
Colored Prisms on the Floor, *Meg Gagnon* 81

A Supermarket Supply of Delight,   *Lynda Calabrese* 84
Elegy for Nannie,   *Janet Ruth Heller* 89
A Vanishing Breed,   *Joan Kramer* 91
My Heart Knows,   *Amy J. Gup* 93
Mildy's Attic,   *Carole Bellacera* 95
In Memory of Claudia Harris,   *Ingrid Reti* 100
Slice,   *Jenna Day* 103
Adoration,   *Ayesha Maqueda Vashti* 105
For the Lady Who Never Screamed at Me
    and Smelled of Sugar,   *Dorothy Peterson Cooke* 108
Remembering Mamie,   *Patricia Smith Ranzoni* 109

NO FEAR OF WHAT NEEDS DOING
I Send You Word,   *Darcy Gottlieb* 115
My Grandmother's Hands,   *Carol Barrett* 117
Waiting for Your Birthday,   *Barbara J. Mayer* 120
Legacy of Love,   *Louise Hess* 121
Even the Birds,   *Sarah Singer* 124
Tea in the Parlor or Fish for Breakfast,   *Annette Johns* 125
Contradictions,   *Anne Scott* 128
When I was Twelve, My Grandmother Died,   *Margie Lee Gallagher*   133
High Standards,   *Ruth H. Kuehler* 134
Keepsakes,   *Cherise Wyneken* 138
The Strength of the Cat,   *Kathleen M. McNamara* 139
Homemaker,   *Cinda Thompson* 142
Her Intensity was Slender and Silent,   *Joan Payne Kincaid* 144
Cotton Balls and Mysticism,   *Wayt Hamill* 146

A SUDDEN SENSE OF HER
Grandma Bessie,   *Barbara Foster* 153
Coda,   *Robin Dellabough* 155
Amateurs,   *Denise Low* 156
Become Your Bubbe,   *Elaine Starkman* 157
Where My Grandmother Laughs,   *Joanna M. Weston* 159
The Jewel,   *Rona Spalten* 160
Loose Photograph,   *Robin Greene* 163
Shadowy Corners,   *Marilyn Reynolds* 164
Her Silence,   *Ruth Daigon* 167
The Old Country,   *Rosemund Handler* 169
Of Time and Place,   *Chalise Miner* 171

In Memory of Rose, *Jackie Fox* 172
Geraniums, *Meleta Murdock Baker* 174
Mary Hynes Remembered, *Joyce McMillin Everett* 175
After the Stroke, *Geraldine Zeigler* 176
The Game, *Sarah Singer* 177
The Much of Her, *Susan Brunn-Puett* 178
Missouri Twilight, *Lynn Buck* 179
Grandma, I Too am a Grandma, *Joanne Seltzer* 182
Requiem, *Joanne Seltzer* 183
The New Bathing Suit, *Marguerite Hiken* 184
The Mustard Seed, *Monika John* 187

Photo Credits 190

There are blank pages at the end of each section of the book. You may wish to use these to personalize FILTERED IMAGES by the addition of your own writings, photos or pen and ink drawings that capture your family's unique history.

WAITING FOR THEM TO SPEAK

A PORTRAIT/
A COLLAGE
Marian Olson

Grandmothers. Mine were lost
in the family tree long before
I was conceived, along with the
sound of their voices, their dreams
and disappointments. Mother,
a single woman orphaned at three,
brought no memories of her mother,
no skeletons or stories, no pretty songs—
nothing, but iron values and a will
big enough to raise three girls
on her own, while working two jobs.
And her mother or my dead father's
mother, *who was she?* I'd like to
believe she was quick as her wit,
and generous, with a curious mind.
A woman who honored the earth,
knew the way of the stars, and could read.
She would play Chopin on a spinet,
well enough to please herself or any
other listening ear. Early mornings
before the sun clapped its hands
and the rooster crowed, she would
light the fires and dip into the water
bucket, stirring up magic in cast iron
pots on a wooden stove.
She'd know the pleasure of gathering
warm and delicate eggs,
the sweat of working the hoe,
furrowing, seeding, and gathering
a harvest, which sometimes failed—
and when it did she could bear it
without blame, pick up and begin again.
And when the sky bulged purple
and winds shreiked like witches
in the yellow corn and poplars
swayed, she wouldn't think of hiding

9

like a baby in the darkest place,
she would stand on the porch outside,
hands braced on aproned hips
and laugh, facing the wind.

MARIAN OLSON, author of *Facing the Wind* (Raven Press) lives in the high desert of California where she teaches creative writing. Her second book, *Songs of the Chicken Yard*, is a collection of haiku/senyru and is forthcoming in 1992. She is currently working on a collection of goddess poems.

GRANDMOTHER I NEVER KNEW
Elaine Starkman

an old woman
a busy Jewish
woman with fine wrinkles
light eyes like mine
not mamma's or papa's
left-handed
sloppy like me

who was born nine
months after her death
who I've heard
about all my life
how I move like her
when I half-heartedly
sweep or cook

a landlady locked in a city
collecting rent and stray dogs
mumbling prayers
she doesn't believe

a character in a case book
who dreams of yellow flowers
in yellowed photographs
of the old country of lost loves
fading under a glass frame
on a parlor buffet

this singular woman
so boastful of her learning
the grandmother
I never knew

Both the prose and the poetry of ELAINE STARKMAN have been published extensively. Long a teacher of writing, she has recently edited *Without a Single Answer: Poems on Contemporary Israel* (Magnes Museum, Berkeley, 1990). The Walnut Creek, California resident has just herself become a grandma.

THE PHOTOGRAPH
Dee Burnlees

Trapped in black and white
square jaw determined
to make the most of life's joys
laughing, loving every moment
beloved by mate, son, grandson
and now by me—a stranger.

You would have taken my hand
declaring, pleased,
"This is my granddaughter"
kissing my forehead
a welcome blessing
—if you had known.

I came from another
secretly
raised in ignorance
of real roots
those genetic arteries
of identity.

Too late I find you grandmother
I can only know
what they choose to tell me
and what your face whispers
every time I pass you on the wall
"We are the same."

DEE BURNLEES of Hepworth, Ontario, writes about family relationships that develop
when a forty-eight-year-old adoptee finds her birth family. She also spins and weaves
by the shores of Lake Huron when she is not tending the library of the elementary school
where she teaches.

DEBT
Sharon Parten Gaskill

So much I don't know
Was it dark then?
   nurse gone for the day
    you, full and young,
     on the hard edge,
      table draped already
       in white
      your gown hanging on you
        like a shroud
        white, the better for bleaching.

Outside, green blades pushing
   up through the cold earth
    relentless
within
   the smell of alcohol
    honed steel and towels
     on the tray
   a basin on the floor.

Was your mother there?
   small bird,
    heart taut with fear and love.

What was it, made you stay his hand?
   dark angel at the door
   bright flash of future
    in the growing dusk
   outcry of heart: no more invasion,
    desolation
  a riot in the blood?

For all the nights that followed
   at a life's throw—
    fireflies in the country
     shooting stars
      breeze through the open windows,
   La Traviata in the darkened hall
    I in silken green and gold,

you in fur-wrapped burgundy—
and even in the chapel's dark,
white gown lying
lace down on the wooden pew,
I too old to cry
and you too kind to tell me—

How could I have guessed?
you, who held my hand through childhood's scrapes,
youth's hurricanes
who set me on the soft shore
of your lap, your love,
indulgences
my head harbour,
within whose reach
no harm could come—

that you sat once
on a spring night
alone with life and death
and chose my father's life,
a life as hard as death to carry,
you, who never told me.

SHARON PARTEN GASKILL lives in San Antonio, Texas, with her husband Hal, daughter Anne and son Hol. She has written poems and children's books and is working on a screenplay on the transformations of motherhood. *Debt* is for Eunice Parten Slaughter, whose giving has known no bounds.

PORTRAITS: FOREMOTHERS
Jane Hill Purtle

They hang in the portrait gallery of my life. I look long into their faces, waiting for them to speak, but they are mute. Many days pass, and I gaze again at their faces, holding my granddaughter by the hand. The pictures mesmerize us; they are our flesh, our blood, but they are silent.

Then, I begin to speak, my thoughts and feelings of all the past days becoming words:

Mary B. Dill (1849-1913), I have copies of your marriage license to my great-grandfather John dated April 11, 1868 and the accompanying affidavit attesting that you were eighteen years old when you married. These legal documents are the first of several I have collected from your history. They are practically all I know of your life, but they tell me you were a fighter for rights and property. I wonder if great-grandfather tired of your demands and left you to raise the family alone, or if you were forced to fight for your rights and learned to demand what you needed. I want to believe about you what I believe about myself—that you fought for your marriage but had to give it up when the compromises were too great.

You didn't know much about John when you married him, certainly didn't know that his father had had five wives and abandoned John's mother after the Civil War. Your John also had restless urges. In 1895 he announced that he was leaving, the marriage was over, he wanted his freedom.

I can imagine the day it happened because in 1975, eighty years later, I played the same scene. I was folding clothes early one morning in the family room when John, *my* John, walked through. I was holding a yellow towel in my hand when he called from the bathroom, "I plan to move out in two or three weeks."

"What do you mean, move out?" I stiffened.

"I don't love you any more," he said. "I haven't loved you for years. I've been thinking about this for a long time."

In the next few weeks I pleaded and promised and cried. I lost ten pounds in ten days. But he left.

When your John left, you made sure he left with nothing except a few hundred dollars. Both of you signed the deed giving all your land to my grandmother and the other minor children. You never saw him again, but you heard that he had another family in Louisiana.

You took up your life, kept your children close by, and doted on your grandchildren, so much that you deeded your entire estate to one of them. So it took another lawsuit after your death to clear up that problem.

But your story didn't end with your death. In 1933, twenty years afterward, John returned to Bullard, to the homeplace—in his casket—and was buried beside you at Mixon. Your story was complete.

Complete and yet not complete. I look into your eyes and wonder what you gave me, what I still need to learn from you, what you would say to me if you could speak. Why are women rejected by the men they trust? Why do relationships fail and women are left behind with a handful of broken pieces? What can I tell my daughter and my granddaughter to protect them from being pierced to the quick by the sharp, jagged edges?

This second portrait is the only great-grandmother I ever saw. Her face is stern, unsmiling; her shoulders straight and commanding. Earnestine Matilda Augier Hill Curley (1853-1941), my father describes you as the best woman he ever knew.

At three, you left Marseilles, France, in a ship bound for New Orleans. I don't know if you ever became a U.S. citizen, but you lived through a traumatic period of your adopted country's history: the Civil War, Reconstruction, the Spanish-American War, World War I, and Hitler's invasion of Europe.

While the world struggled with its problems, you birthed ten children by two husbands, neither of whom lived to see all their children born. When your first husband, my great-grandfather Matthew, was shot to death in a hunting accident, leaving you pregnant with your sixth child, I can imagine the heartache and fear you felt.

It was 1880. What does a young widow with small children and no skills do in 1880? You married a second time, but he was a fugitive from justice, as you later learned. So when he died in 1886, you moved, with the five living children of your first marriage and the three children of your second marriage and pregnant again, back home to relatives and made it the best you could. You became strong and good.

When your children began having children, you were busy as ever. You were present at the birth of every grandchild, and 1913 kept you busy. Four grandchildren had already arrived when my grandmother Lura anxiously awaited your coming on November 28 for the birth of my dad. You were tired, but your daughter-in-law Lura was not strong and she needed your help and encouragement. You brought along little hand-stitched caps and blankets to greet the new baby, caps and blankets that I am keeping for my own granddaughter.

Even when you could no longer live alone, you maintained your own quarters in your daughter's home—a room immaculately clean and ordered for your use. There you welcomed your grandchildren, taught them to say "yes, ma'am" and "no sir." There, you patched and mended hundreds of pants, shirts, socks for your children and grandchildren, making tiny, beautiful stitches, so tiny it was hardly possible to tell they had been patched.

Grandmother Earnestine, I look at your portrait. Your erect posture and stern, firm expression tell me that you have an unbending will. I admire your independence, your energy, your ability to endure, but I wonder what you and I would talk about today. Would I still be afraid of you as I was years ago? Could you understand that, even as a woman, I need to cry? That I hurt so much sometimes that I bend in the storm and almost break? I will never be as strong and good as you and I wonder why.

Mary Jane Dill Atkins (1882-1916), I have part of your name, but I never saw you. Your picture tells me that you like tailored clothes and practical hairdos. You grew up without a father, never saw him to remember him. So you became strong and independent and did not have to have a man to hitch up your buggy or wring a chicken's neck. You married my grandpa when you were twenty and already expecting your first child. You were practical and efficient, not inclined to pet or touch your children, but they were well cared for, well fed, strong and capable like you.

Whenever Grandpa Sim retreated to the back pasture and didn't want to go gallivanting across the country to see relatives, you hitched up the team, bundled the six kids into the back of the wagon, and took off for a weekend with your in-laws in Bullard.

Then the in-laws came to repay the visit. It was a busy time getting ready for them—pies to bake; chickens to kill, pluck, and cut up; greens to pick, wash, and cook. The oldest two boys helped on the promise that they could play with their cousins Walter and Marvin when the family arrived.

On Saturday night everyone sat around the table.

"Pass the mashed potatoes—and some gravy, too," Cousin Walter said.

"This is the best fried chicken I ever tasted. Jane, how do you do it?" The sister-in-law's praise was especially welcome.

"Aunt Jane, could I have another biscuit—and the blackberry jelly? This is my last one—'til breakfast."

"You've outdone yourself tonight," Sim said.

When they left Sunday afternoon, you were tired and happy, with a sort of glow inside, happy that everybody in both families had a good time and enjoyed the food.

Grandmother Jane, I wish you had not died so many years ago. I know your children missed your comforting presence. Even today my own mother says, with tears in her eyes, "I can't remember how mother's face looked, but I remember the day she died and how my brother cried." Think what we could have shared if you had lived—sitting around the kitchen table, drinking tea and exchanging recipes. Why does death take from us gifts we never get to open, friendships we can never enjoy, and warm bodies we can never touch, leaving us only a name and a picture?

We turn to the last portrait and look long into the beautifully pensive face.

Lura M. Smith Hill (1892-1921), you are the other half of my name, a name full of music and mystery. Your life is a puzzle whose pieces I cannot fit together. At nineteen you married my Grandpa Ozark, thirty-five years old, hot tempered and obstinate. You were shy, quiet, afraid, compliant to his demands and expectations. Four babies came quickly, and then the last one, Joseph, died while you were still nursing him. Some say you gave him an overdose of turpentine when he was sick with the croup. Then you went to the asylum, but grandpa brought you home. You grieved and tried to care for your three little ones. Another baby came and then for months you lay on your bed in a darkened room. Your sister sat beside your bed and held your hand as the music faded.

Why did you give up and leave four children behind to grow to adulthood without a mother? I understand that you were soft and pliable, easily damaged, and the pain was intense. Pain—much more pain than you could bear alone and no one to bear it for you. More pain than I want to consider or ponder. I did not know your story when I put aside your name and chose Grandmother Jane for my namesake. But now, knowing, I still cannot be present to your pain and bear it. I cannot understand the mystery of your life, not do I yet weep for you. Perhaps some day I can.

As my voice fades, I wait for my foremothers to speak, hoping that they will tell me that they know me, know my story better than I know theirs, better than I know it myself. I try to catch their eyes across the gulf. But they are silent, as I feel the gentle pressure of my granddaughter's hand within mine.

LURA JANE HILL PURTLE lives in East Texas, the setting of *Foremothers*. She teaches English at a Methodist junior college and is the author of a family history cookbook, *Food from the Hills*. The granddaughter of the sketch is part of the dream yet to be realized.

GRANDMOTHER'S EYES
Ingrid Reti

You were my father's mother
I never knew you.
Today I found your picture
looked at you
enclosed in your bronzed frame;
erect, proud woman
wearing
a black lace blouse
with high, frilly collar
supporting your double chin.

My eyes traveled slowly
past your closed lips
wide nose, smooth round cheeks
to your eyes
and suddenly
you ceased to be a stranger.

Those eyes are eyes
that daily greet me
in the mirror.

INGRID RETI is a literature and creative writing instructor at California Polytechnic State University, Extended Education in San Luis Obispo, California. She produces and hosts a weekly TV show *On Books and Authors*. Her poetry has appeared in numerous literary magazines. *Echoes of Silence*, her second collection of poetry, was published in 1990.

SEPIA TONE: *Helen Marie, 1840-1898*
Rosalie MacCary

I see the sadness in your eyes,
The camera caught and fixed the pain;
You wept, but no one heard your cries.

The smile is slight, does not disguise
The haunted look you can't contain.
I see the sadness in your eyes.

Aloof, your husband seldom tries
To understand if you complain.
You wept, but no one heard your cries.

You hold the infant while it dies.
And forty-five, with child again,
I see the sadness in your eyes.

Now sick to death, ill health denies
Old age, the peace you longed to gain.
You wept, but no one heard your cries.

Too late to hear your dreams, your sighs,
With death your secrets must remain.
I see the sadness in your eyes;
You wept, but no one heard your cries.

ROSALIE MacCARY lives in Spokane, Washington, with her husband Lawrence. In recent months she has become a grandmother, attended a 40-year high school reunion and received an M.F.A. in creative writing from Eastern Washington University.

THE LIZARDS AND THE WORMS
Nancy Kay Webb

Early in the morning of the day I was born, so early that it still was dark, my grandmother sat at a round table in the back yard trying to read the morning paper. Fully dressed she sat, straining her eyes to read the editorial page of the *Fort Worth Star Telegram*. The pre-dawn dark was very, very dark, but if she held the page at just the right angle she could catch a ray or two of light from the street lamp beyond the low garden wall. Then by bringing her face as close to the paper as possible without interrupting the gentle beam of light, she could make out the words.

So, trying her best to read in the dark, my grandmother sat, encircled by the invisible green of my grandfather's garden, and the contrapuntal chirping of all its summer crickets. While indoors my grandfather bustled about, busy with many things that probably didn't need to be done.

❖❖❖

She slides my high chair up to a white board. White teeth farther than I can reach on either side of me. Black ones, also. Two and three, two and three. I slap and pat. Is this a plaything just for me? I'll slap and pat for as long as they leave me here...

When grandmother sat down to the piano, she sat with her hips on the very edge of the piano bench, her right foot on the pedal, her left foot back, resting on its toes. She sat with her spine rigid and her ample torso inclined toward the keyboard.

She played rather poorly, though. Her music shuffled. It stuttered. It was never up to the level of grandfather's. With his flute grandfather made silver music, a smooth, gleaming thread of ice that wound around and around grandmother's lack of dexterity.

These two reared me, my grandmother and my grandfather. Grandfather quit his job to take care of me. He stayed home while grandmother taught civics at the junior college.

Grandfather watched over me with great care. If I stayed in the bathroom a long time he knocked on the door to tell me to get off the toilet. Sitting on the toilet too long, he said, could give me hemorrhoids. He wouldn't let me wander in the alley behind his garden. He wouldn't let me eat anything that had fallen on the ground. He wouldn't let me swim in public pools. Sometimes I was tormented by his worries yet I always felt loved and safe. Always. But grandmother...Something about grandmother disturbed me, made me uneasy.

A full length mirror on a closet door. The door a little bit open. In the mirror I see rising up from the heavy, dark bed large, white vegetable folds of smooth flesh. I'm scared, but I won't move, won't keep walking or pull my eyes away. So white...Full flesh doubling back on itself—not just once but more than once. She doesn't see me. Her eyes look into a stillness in the mirror as she polishes cream into the folds of her flesh. The white underside of a magnolia.

❖❖❖

Grandfather's garden was never still. The slightest ripple of air set in motion thousands of leaves, and these, in turn, sent hundreds of thousands of diamonds jumping and rolling along the ground. Everything moved; flowers opened and closed with the sun. Creatures flew. Creatures made homes in the black earth.

There was only one spot in the garden I didn't love—a shady corner, the corner farthest from the back door. Hanging there was a large old bell. Vines had crawled up the wooden post to the bell. Their tendrils had coiled around the clapper, strangling it to silence. No amount of tugging at the bell rope could make it ring.

I hated this corner of the garden, was afraid of the things that might be hiding there. Grandmother didn't understand this. No matter what, she never could have understood. *She has something to show me. With a happy voice she calls, "Come here, Minta." But she's standing in the hated corner. "No," I say from my safe place under a low, blinking tree—a tree with flowers like bunches of grapes. "Don't be silly," she says. "This is something you might never again get a chance to see. Hurry!" But I ask, "What is it?" This makes her cross. She doesn't say so but I know. "You'll have to see for yourself," she says. She doesn't understand! Why can't she understand?*

Then a bee in a purple flower scares me. She won't want to hear about that either.

There was much too much she didn't understand...

During my first year at grammar school grandfather developed a gall stone and had to spend several days in the hospital, and I remember grocery shopping with grandmother. She didn't understand how to grocery shop. I tried to tell her, while we stood with the oranges on one side of us and two kinds of lettuce on the other side. I tried to explain that she must make a list and that this list must be in order of the store's layout. "Grandfather says a person spends one dollar for every minute he stays in the store," I told her. She stood there, short and dumpy, with elbows gray from leaning on so many newspapers. She stood looking at me. She looked at me for so long that I felt the lizards and worms begin to cringe, begin to look toward the oranges and dripping lettuce leaves for sanctuary. Then for just a split second she closed her cloudy gray eyes. When she opened them again she was focused on something else, and down the aisle she pushed the hobbling shopping cart with its broken wheel. She clumped her way through the store, picking up whatever she pleased, not reading labels, not even ignoring a free sample from the woman with the white apron and the electric skillet.

"Don't you know that free samples and store music are just to keep you here longer? A person spends a whole dollar for every minute he stays in the store!" I felt like crying. I felt unsafe.

❖❖❖

I don't remember exactly when Julian moved in next door, but at some point he was there with his two flutes, his piano, and his electronic tuner. He was half the age of my grandparents but he spent most of his spare time with them, came over often to play music, to lament the artistic wasteland of the U.S.A. in general and the Southwest in particular.

Grandfather and Julian played duets by Bach, Purcell, Couperin. Sometimes they included grandmother and did simpler pieces for two flutes and piano. Always I was there on the couch listening.

But sometimes Julian played his flute alone. He blew long, low sounds, painful tones I heard with my throat. Then he might suddenly slide all the way to the top of his voice and strike there again and again. Pip. Pip. Pip. Or hold one note for a long time, for too long, rubbing it all over with his lips, stretching it as far as it could go in every direction. This wasn't like grandfather's music. Grandfather's music was clean. It was the pattern of an oriental rug, of light coming through the blinds. Julian's music wasn't clean. It was unhealthy, like the unhealthy night air.

I wanted to be rude to Julian. I wanted to tell him, "You don't know a thing about music!" I began complaining about his visits. I began refusing to run next door to bring back A-440's for my grandfather.

Julian's eyes are too black. His flute hurts my throat.

It's night. His voice wakes me up. It comes from the tangled corner of the garden. Grandmother's voice rises up beside it. I can't hear what they're saying. Is she showing him those things I'm never able to see: a bear, a hunter, ladles in different sizes? No, or else they would sit in an open place.

Grandfather snores in the next room. What are they saying? Their voices rise up through the dark like the smell of flowers. I hold my breath, but still can't catch the words. Their talking moves up like music—no words. I hold my breath. My heart thumps in my head. I'll never forgive her for this. My grandmother.

One Sunday afternoon when it looked like it was going to storm and grandfather was busy in the garden trying to get the jonquil bulbs set before the rain started, grandmother told me she was going next door to listen to Julian play for a while. I began to cry.

"There, there, child," she said, sitting down beside me on the bed. "What's the matter?"

But I wouldn't soften to her. "You'd better not go! You'd better not go!" I screamed it over and over again until she stood up and began brushing her hair again.

I cried and screamed so loudly that grandfather came indoors. First he scolded grandmother for ignoring me and then he said to me, "There, there, now, you're too big a girl to carry on like this. If you don't like jazz, you don't have to listen to it. You and I'll just stay right here, all cozy and nice, where we don't have to listen…"

But I did have to listen. I had to open my bedroom window and listen as hard as I could through the screen, listen as hard as I could, holding my breath whenever the noise of my breathing drew a film over the notes. Listen as hard as I could, stopping my heart if it got out of rhythm with the music.

There there, now.

The rain starts. I hear the fat drops slapping the ground under my window. More and more and more until it crackles like fire.

The rain falls then like pain. It closes me in, cuts me off from everything. It's beyond my control. It falls like the dark pain of dreams.

On the other side of this water things go on. Things I can't control. A man with black eyes plays his flute. His music wraps up those who listen, includes those around him in exactly the way I'm not included. In exactly the way I'm cut off. And all this is beyond my control.

❖❖❖

Four o'clock in the morning and grandfather up with every light in the house on. Nothing would do but he'd have me up, too. Grandmother was gone. Grandfather wept. He wept for days and days. But I didn't. She'd never fit in here, not really.

She sent us cards from Paris, Brussels, Berlin, Dresden and Warsaw. Then came a pitiful letter from Julian. She had left him, deserted him, he said, for his uncle. She had eloped to Morocco with his uncle and he, Julian, was a broken man. His life had no meaning now. Could he come live with grandfather and me? He begged this, he said, on his knees. He threw himself at our mercy.

Grandfather was glad. He'd brightened at the prospect of Julian's company. I believed he was going to say yes! I flung myself down on the rug and screamed and shrieked until grandfather shushed me and promised that it wouldn't happen. He'd tell Julian to find some other place to live.

Grandmother didn't write again. Nor did Julian. And at length grandfather finished his weeping. We tried to go back to living our days and nights as we always had. Now I'm middle-aged and grandfather is dead.

❖❖❖

I've been provided for yet left in want. I live day to day cut off from everything. At night I can't sleep. In the morning I roam the house, dusting table tops and vases, cleaning the Persian rugs. I sit down to play the piano. Occasionally I'll sing a few lieder. Whenever the weather doesn't forbid it, I come out here to the garden where I see grandmother sitting at this very table reading the morning paper. I can see her sitting here just as I can see her squatting over there trying to show me something. What was it? I never found out. I stood apart from her, curious but afraid of the complicated vegetation in that corner of the garden, afraid of what might be hiding there, afraid of the mute bell. Safely I stood under the wisteria tree. There were spangles of light in my eyes, and I asked her, "What is it?" But she insisted I see for myself, promised it was something special, something remarkable. Still I was afraid. So while she coaxed, I stood quietly, lost to the mosaic of my eyes. Until a bee chased me out into the bright light of the afternoon.

What was it she wanted to show me? I wonder about it. I wonder, too, if for me it would have made any sort of difference.

NANCY KAY WEBB of Point Arena, California, claims that her grandmother is "the most wonderful grandmother in the world" and that *The Lizards and the Worms* is most decidedly not about her. This work of fiction explores the sort of grandmother its author might have become had she remained in Texas and been confronted with the task of raising such a child as Minta.

TO THOSE I NEVER KNEW
Janet Overmyer

What were you like,
You, known to me only from bits of family lore?
My father's mother—tiny, married to a tyrant,
Always pregnant, nursing, or miscarrying,
Finally mother of—how many?
None of the five grown survivors was sure.
My mother's mother—Norwegian, with a much older Norwegian mate,
Mother of two daughters
Whom she did not cuddle, or praise, or even touch,
Yet gentle.

Both women much adored by their son and daughter, my parents—
Perhaps too much, causing marriage friction
As each partner sought futilely for the mother's perfection in the other—?
Are you both sainted beyond sanity?
Did you destroy my parents' union?

Am I at all like you, my unknown forebears?
I, who never married, nor gave birth?
I who am far from sainthood?

I must have inherited something from someone—
My love for animals, books, music,
My teaching skills,
My writing—
Also my stubbornness, my loneliness,
My lack of love?

I will never know just what was your bequest
Except for your most precious gift:
Life.

JANET OVERMYER has published fiction, nonfiction, poetry and book reviews; she
has also had plays performed. She is an instructor in the Department of English, Ohio
State University, and is owned by Dana, Caitlin, Molly and Ashley, the four most
beautiful cats in Columbus.

GRANDMA MERTA AND ME
Joyce McMillin Everett

Here we stand in this photo
Hand in hand
Staring at the camera
Barely smiling
All effort
Concentrated
On the "don't squint"
Order from my mother
The photographer.
The early eastern sunlight
Sears our retinas
As we strain
To hold our lids open
And unblinking.
The picture is important
For both of us
Merta at seventy; me at six.
Wearing starched cotton dresses
Ironed to absolute smoothness
Our black shoes polished
Her hair a perfect white cloud
Mine slicked into braids,
We're aware of our infrequent visits.
There's no dropping in for lunch.
It takes a long vacation
And days of travel
To cover the miles
From New York to Iowa.
So our hands grip
And we hold the pose
Trying for the perfect picture
To catch the memory
Of our last day together.

JOYCE McMILLIN EVERETT was born in Waterloo, Iowa, grew up in Endicott, New York, and currently lives in Hampton Bays, New York, with her husband James. She apportions creative energy to writing desk, pottery studio and flower gardens with frequent time out for family and friends. She credits the six years of monthly meetings with her women writers' group for much of her growth as a poet.

CAMEO
Delores Goodrick Beggs

Spring.
About now, grandma
would be asking mam
if we could come
help with the cleaning.

The yearly ritual begun,
like gladioli blooming in sequence,
mam spoke faintly of bother.
"Nonsense!" Grandma's cheery eyes
met my sister's, mine, beamed
her secret smile
that promised fantasy
among the dusty chests
stored in neat rows
in grandma's attic.

About now,
grandma's watching eyes would sparkle,
she'd chirp "Wanda's silk for you?
That was a gel!"
at my sister,
and on me, her namesake
parading in grandma's old party dress
unfolded fresh from its tissue wrapping,
she'd fasten tear-blurred
speculative glance.

DELORES GOODRICK BEGGS of Milpitas, California, is a columnist for two magazines—*Midnight Zoo,* a science-fiction, fantasy and horror semi-pro magazine, and *Experience Unlimited Writers and Artists Organization* (EUWAO), a writer's market news publication. She is working on the sequel to her young people's fantasy book, *Myrfa C'an and the Edgestones.*

LILLIAN
Lynn Buck

She's not like any other grandma you ever saw, my grandma Lillian. She has beautiful yellow curly hair and likes to blow bubbles with purple gum. She taught us how, me and my little sister, when we visited her last summer. She wears gorgeous silky dresses and open-toed shoes with high heels and lots of bangly gold bracelets and dangly earrings and red nail polish and make-up which our other grandma doesn't at all, not even lipstick. And she smells like springtime with lilacs in bloom. She talks different than anyone we know here in Kansas City and when she laughs it's bright and fizzy like a Cherry Pepsi.

Daddy brought us to Long Island and left mommy crying at home, but Grandma Lillian insisted that he had to send for her. "Call her and patch things up," she said, "so our whole family can be together." Her voice was firm as a rock and her eyes were shooting sparks. We learned right away you don't talk her out of anything once her mind is made up.

She doesn't pray to Jesus like we do. She prays in a synagogue like daddy used to do before he was baptized and born again. But I don't see how such a nice person could go to hell where the Bible says folks will go who don't believe in Jesus.

One day she bought us bubble pipes and took a picture of us blowing the most beautiful soap bubbles all shimmery and full of rainbows, hundreds of them floating around our heads and into the geraniums on the terrace. She put the picture in a silver frame on her desk. She says we are the spitting image of her two daughters, our aunts, when they were little and sometimes she forgets and calls us Becky and Lisa instead of our real names.

Another day she took us to the beach where my sister cried because the big waves scared her but I was not a bit afraid even when I got a mouthful of salty water. I was only six then. We held hands and bounced in the waves together, me and Grandma Lillian.

She says she's sixty years old but you wouldn't believe it if you saw her. She calls us on the phone just about every week but that's not the same as being there, and I don't know when we will ever go back because daddy says it's too expensive and besides if we see too much of Grandma Lillian we might forget all about Jesus and that would be a mortal sin.

LYNN BUCK of Hampton Bays, New York, is Missourian by birth and disposition. Her work has appeared in many national journals and anthologies including *Poets for Africa* and *The Tie that Binds*. She has published a volume of poems, *Autumn Fires*, and has completed a novel tentatively titled *Antiques Are Rarely Perfect*.

THE TENDER HEART
Alice E. Sink

Picture granny's kitchen in late October. An afternoon more than fifteen years ago—gone—except for the final sunbeams still playing on the marble mint slab. The wood stove boasts a five-gallon pot of stewed chicken and dumplings floating on globules of chicken fat. The oblong oak table is set for supper. Three places, one for each of us—me, granny, and my daddy, who will be home tonight and tomorrow night before he starts out on another selling trip.

Old Mutt, granny's collie, meets my bus at the end of the dirt driveway and noses my hand as we walk together to the back door. I see the light from the bare bulb through the window and know granny is in the kitchen. She is sitting on one of the kitchen chairs with her back to the door, and her left foot is bare and propped on the stubby green footstool we use as a stepladder in the pantry. She is working on her corn. "Mary Ruth, close that door tight, you hear, girl," she says. "We ain't planning on heatin' the outside this winter." She doesn't look up.

"Yes-ma'am," I chant and stop to hang my jacket on the wooden peg beside the wood box. "That ol' corn bothering you again, granny?"

She looks at me. I can tell she hurts because her cheekbones shine with the tears. She looks back down at her toe and continues working on the corn. Her fingernails are broken and thick; with her right thumbnail, she gouges at the target on the inside of her little toe. "I ain't seeming to be doing no good with this confounded thing," she swears as she holds and digs and scrapes. "Mrs. Johnson says maybe it's what you call a soft corn 'cause once you get going good trying to get the gristle out, you run into soft tender skin." Stooped over the footstool, granny stops only long enough to push back strands of reddish hair that fall from the knot on her neck.

"Ain't there some kind of medicine or salve you can put on them things to be rid of 'em?" I feel I must offer encouragement as long as I stand there and watch. Maybe something I say will stop her tears.

"Stand over this-a-way, Mary Ruth," she says. "You're in my light."

"You know, like fatback on warts, or something like that," I volunteer, adjusting myself a few inches back so my shadow won't be on granny's foot. "There must be something."

Granny props her foot at a different angle and starts to dig again with her nail. "That nice man down at the drugstore said white iodine might help, and it did seem to make the core somewhat harder—but it's the soft skin around the kernel that keeps giving me problems," she says, her lips forming an I-really-don't-know-what-else-to-do response. "If it wasn't for the softness, I'd have this jackleg out in no time a'tall, but don't you worry none, Mary Ruth, you're too young to be a'frettin' over me."

I was nine years young that winter, and granny was fifty-something. My mother had died of a heart attack and left me and my daddy to move in with granny so she could look after me while my daddy travelled. And look after me, she did. School during the day was okay, but afternoons and evenings with granny were soft and easy and warm.

We played go fishing in front of the blazing fire. Granny sat on one side of the little table, her foot soaking in the enamel pan of steaming boric acid water, while I sat on the side next to the radio so I could turn the dial to our favorite gospel music. Granny patted her lame foot, and the swish of the water lapping on the rim of the pan kept time with the tune coming from the radio shows. Many times, just as I was thinking hard about what to discard, granny would let out a shrill cry, arch her back, and pat her foot even harder. "What's the matter, granny?" I screamed, terrified that God was going to take granny like He took my mother.

"Ain't nothing, precious, but that dad-blamed, confounded pain shootin' through my toe," she spewed with a vengeance that I now associate with acquaintances' clenched-teeth damn-it-to-hells. "I declare," granny uttered, half in apology for the attention she had attracted, "I do believe it couldn't hurt any more if somebody took an ice pick and gouged in that toe. Are you going to discard, or not?"

After the card games, we popped corn, using the wire popper with the extra long handle my daddy had made from an old fire poker. "Don't eat them kernels that ain't popped, Mary Ruth," granny scolded. "Them things'll lay in your stomach like bullets. Besides that, you'll break off your teeth trying to crunch 'em. Now stop it." So I'd sneak a pocketful of scorched half-cooked kernels for later when granny wasn't looking.

Granny's health was unusually good for a fifty-year-old woman, and the only affliction she could boast was her corn. Mrs. Sadie Johnson and granny would get on the telephone and talk for hours about their ailments, but granny always refused to let Mrs. Johnson get the best of her. She would hang up the receiver, turn to me, and, hands on hips, the canvas bedroom shoes scuffing on the linoleum rug, demand, "Now, child, what do you think of a woman who thinks she's got worse than this-here corn?" Before she gave me time to answer, she started in, "I ask you. In all honesty. Can anybody else predict when it's gonna rain? Can anybody else tell when we're gonna have day after day of snow? Of course not. Only me."

And snow it did. Granny could predict right down to the very day. When the drifts piled up against the back door, me and granny would hook a thick cord to her aluminum roaster pan, which we filled with chicken feed. We'd get dressed up warm, with granny pulling a pair of rubber boots over her canvas bedroom shoes, and go to the chicken lot to feed the hens and Rooster Red. On the way back to the house, we stopped at the woodpile and I'd load the roaster pan with firewood while granny picked up kindling stored in the shed. Old Mutt sensed the frivolity of the evening and joined in when I dared roll down the snow-covered bank that in the summer housed granny's blue ribbon marigolds. "I'm goin' on in the house, Mary Ruth," granny shouted as I slid down the bank one last time. "Bring Mutt and put him on the back porch for the night. And don't forget that roaster pan." Her reminders echoed through the icy tree branches. I knew heaven must be like this.

But the first warm spring morning my daddy told granny to be dressed and waiting at 2:30. He'd made her an appointment with the foot doctor in Galax to have her corn cut out. "I ain't going through another winter seeing you drag one half-naked foot around the house. We'll get that thing gone forever." Poking around on the sideboard for his wallet and keys, he turned and said to me, as if an afterthought: "And you can go, too, Mary Ruth, if I need help getting granny up and down any kind of steps."

I looked at granny, who had stopped washing up the breakfast dishes in the enamel pan on the wood stove. Her face showed a mixture of relief and scaredness, like she was glad on one hand to be getting rid of the menace, but terrified of the doctor's knife she had probably visualized a thousand times. All she said was, "Yes, I reckon it's about that time" and then went back to rinsing the silverware in a second pan of hot water.

So granny and me were ready and waiting in the green rockers on the porch when daddy drove up that afternoon. Granny hadn't said much all day, but the way she was dressed up in her Sunday dress and hat made her look like a queen getting ready for some important event. I tried not to look at her feet, but then my curiosity got the best of me and I glanced down when granny was busy pulling dead leaves from her hanging begonia. On her right foot she wore her black leather walking shoe, as she always called the pair of them, but her left foot was covered with the plaid canvas bedroom shoe—complete with the little toe part cut out. She saw me looking down and said, never skipping a beat getting rid of the begonia leaves, "Well, you know, precious, I ain't gonna be able to wear any type of regular fitting shoe after my surgery." The words "my surgery" were spoken with an importance granny usually reserved for "my fruitcakes" or "my garden."

As it turned out, there weren't any steps to have to help granny up and down. The foot doctor's office, out behind Memorial Hospital, was one of those modern buildings with no steps and no window panes. We didn't have to wait any time at all, and before granny could get any more worked up than she was on the trip to Galax, a nurse told her to come on to the back, that the doctor was ready for her. Granny rose from the little settee, twisted her dress where it ought to be, and took off her hat, handing it to me. "Hold this for me please, darlin'," granny said with a tone that was growing more and more important each time she said something. "And don't mash it, you hear."

Daddy and I waited, thumbing through magazines, and once daddy went out in the hallway to catch a smoke. In about twenty minutes or so, the inner sanctum door opened, and the nurse was helping granny by the arm. She still had the black walking shoe on her right foot, but on her left foot, the hole in the toe of her bedroom shoe had been cut out even more and a bump of white gauze and tape popped through the opening like a mummy at attention. "I'm just fine," granny said just as soon as she looked at my face. How 'bout you and your daddy taking me on home now?"

As we rode back to Big Gap, granny told me about how the doctor had tied a big rubber band around her little toe to cut off the blood circulation and then had given her a shot to kill the pain before he started cutting.

"Law, it didn't take him no time a'tall," granny said proudly, "and to think I been dreadin' this thing for so long. If I'd a-known about how painless it all was, well, I'd a'had this little surgery a long time ago."

Daddy was right about granny being able to go and do. From that day on, she went and she did. Just about every afternoon she dressed herself up, put on her black walking shoes, and if she wasn't strutting somewhere, she was hitching a ride with Mrs. Johnson to circle meeting or a quilting party or the Home Demonstration Club. She never did light long enough after that to play me a decent game of go fishing or listen to the Lone Ranger on the radio or stand on the back porch and cheer me and Old Mutt as we rolled down the snow bank.

And so granny was freed of her affliction then and there that May afternoon in the doctor's office behind Memorial Hospital in Galax. While she was gallivanting around town, I had to find something to do, so I began playing with the girls down the road and got jobs babysitting after school. Eventually I went away to college. Now it is years later when I realize the foot doctor, carving that callous bump from granny's little toe, took the first real jab into the tender heart of my girlhood.

ALICE E. SINK teaches creative writing at High Point College in North Carolina. She was selected as one of ten short story writers to participate in the North Carolina Writer Network Writers & Readers Series, and she has been published in numerous literary magazines nationwide.

BRYNA BAS YOSEF HALEVI
Shulamith Surnamer

At the fixed moment in time
when my grandmother died
in the Hebrew Home on Father Divine's once heavenly Hudson Estate
peacefully holding her visiting daughter's hand one last time
faculties failing only after slightly less than
a full 100 years of usage
I could have been found—
as I believe she found me—
innocently sitting in a college library
surrounded by a troika of favorite languages
celebrating The Song of Myself
po-russki, b'ivrit, and the original whitmanesque.
An erudite generalissima in those self-same tongues
and more,
how could she have left this earth
without checking on the favorite ainekal,
only daughter
of her only daughter after four sons?
How could they have told me later that I was not
an official mourner for my third parent,
a sibling cross the span of years with whom
had been shared more than a bedroom TV set.
I saw her once more after her death
on another sidewalkless suburban subdivision street in Connecticut
patiently walking step by step
robed again in a tightly curled black lambskin
good winter coat
coming to the bris of yet another newborn great-grandson,
my cousin's child.
A blink of my eyes and she vanished from sight forever.
Sabta, I know you would be proud and happy
with the great-grandchildren I have given you.
Dare I hope you would feel the same of me?

SHULAMITH SURNAMER lives on a barrier island off the Atlantic seaboard with her husband, two sons and father. A high school English teacher, she has been cited by Poets House as one of the outstanding teachers of poetry in New York City. Her work has appeared in *Crosscurrents, Sing Heavenly Muse* and *Sarah's Daughters Sing*. As poetry editor of *Judi-isms*, she is currently working on a project about Jewish personalities.

GOING TO BED AFTER EIGHT
Lynette Seator

When I was eight grandmother's lost estate settled
her into my room where she came
nightly like a raider lighting on
the top light, letting it shine on.
A flash of her electric hand flooded
the closets of my sleep.
In the glare she shed
housedress and laces,
knelt folded as her white
prayers purled, their
open mouths rounding the bowl of light.

Years after, your illuminations, grandmother,
float up on a sliver of moon.
Against their stare
my night windows blink out. Stitched in black
I thread my way to bed, sink
dreaming deeply
to where you lie among the roots,
hear you sigh
after the light.

LYNETTE SEATOR of Jacksonville, Illinois, has had both poetry and scholarly articles published in small presses and journals. She also teaches at Illinois College where she headed the Spanish Department and received the Distinguished Professor award. *After the Light* (North Woods Press) is her first book of poetry. She recently organized an interdisciplinary symposium in Moscow entitled *New Understandings of the Experience of Women.*

QUIET ROOMS, EMPTY PLACES
Betty Anholt

I turn the shower off
And standing surrounded by white tiles,
    toweling dry
I hear the water in the pipes gurgle, drop, and rattle,
    quick-dripping from the spout.

The drip-drip a tick-tick, a clock.
A mantel clock in a quiet room
A hollow sound in my grandparents' house.

My grandmothers are a mystery.

One died a generation before I was born,
The other I never knew.

My grandfather's second wife
Brought a son
    to her second husband
As he brought my mother,
    a baby,
        to her.
Having both dug graves in youth
They merged measured lives.

Her bathroom tiles were gray, maroon-trimmed.
I had a velvet skirt that rich maroon.
I wore a red soft sweater,
    jewel-necked, and pearled
And felt like a princess at age eight
Until someone said red and purple—
    she's color-blind.

Real tile, nanny had. Not plastic tile. Not linoleum—
    printed or embossed—
    but glossy, baked clay, cloud-swirled and soft gray.
Her bath window overlooked a garage, a garden, and grass
Bounded at the lower end by wires heavy
    with grapes, vines heavy
    with the sweet taste of Concord.
Potato fields on three sides, and the road to Princeton

on the fourth.
The house floated serene, an island above clumped fields.
Brown fields,
> though her garden rainbowed zinnias, snap-beans,
> rhubarb with red-stemmed elephant leaves.

Forbidden fields, unfenced.
Still, I did not go.
Barren fields,
> where I could see miles of rows.

No place to explore—no hidden spot or rabbit holes
Just clods of earth, of rock, and,
> I guess, potatoes.

I preferred to squirrel up the front yard maples
While Nanny tsk-ed about my future.

I remember standing at the bathroom sink, elbows banging
> porcelain awkwardly

While she scrubbed my hands.
Late afternoon,
> in a home-made yellow cotton slip—half-slip—slipped
> under my armpits so its too-long hem would stay hidden.

I loved that slip—crisp and soft,
> a material for royalty.

Yet…it embarrassed me,
> home-sewn, cotton—not tricot and lace like
> everyone had.

She took my hand—reached over me, trapped
> between porcelain and her
> buttressed breasts

Entwined her fingers with mine, her right hand cradled mine
> as her body shelled my back

And she soaped my palm and hers
Enclosed my hand in hers, turning it, laving it, bringing it
> (as though it had no volition on its own)
> to the water to rinse.

And then the other one.
Like rinsing vegetables in the kitchen, perhaps. Gently,
> firmly,
> spots and flecks removed,
>> then set aside.

Staid, proper, corseted, bigoted, proud, pale,
      English-blood she was.
And me, that olive skin,
      looking a right gypsy by summer's end,
      coming down that road.
She'd shake her hairpinned head, a spider-web net imprisoning
      gray-brown hairs
Why would you want to spend your days here? Nothing to do.

Everything.
Roll marbles along the porch.
Pry them back out of half-moon drains as adults
      rock and talk
In white-painted, green-tipped chairs in twilight.
Listen to gossip and katydids, all buzzing gently.
Watch Howdy Doody and some jungle show,
      Ed Sullivan and Gorgeous George, dancing cigarette packs
      on a tiny tube,
As we eat cantaloupe and ice cream
      seated on heavy furniture in a low-ceilinged room.
Read the temperature. Read.
Sambo, Alice, a history of Tennant Church—
      find names of ancestors buried where the
      Battle of Monmouth raged, where
      Molly Pitcher roamed.

Some reading on that porch, but more above it, in the tree.
And later, in the guest room—not the little room with the
      treadle sewing machine and rag rug,
But the guest room to which I graduated, reluctantly,
      at age eight.
Where, behind a slipper chair
      the hat rack held a fox biting its tail
Where the doilied dressers were empty,
      but celluloid dresser sets dressed the doilies
Where I luxuriated in a double bed and read
Agatha Christie novels about mysterious Egyptian digs
And smelled the dirt of the potato fields as
      the dimity curtains moved
And listened to the occasional car go—or come
      down the road and rise that hill

A hill beyond potato fields
The horizon hill.

That staid English lady loved the games.
Chinese checkers, rummy, Scrabble, cards—a shark.
She was good, and taught me, and so was I.
I'd catch her cheating,
        and tell her so.
She loved my cheeky spunk.
I thing she loved me best of all
I think because she knew—
        yes, she knew
        I loved her.
She never really knew
        how much I needed her quiet house
How she filled my empty places.
I think now how her mind emptied those last years
How she shrunk into her self no longer knowing
        those around her.
I hope she re-entered those days of playing cards,
        sorting buttons
        on the openwork crocheted tablecloth, or rocking by the
        African violets
        with mending on her lap.
I'd like that.

BETTY ANHOLT lives in southwest Florida on Sanibel Island and has published in several regional periodicals. Presently working on her second novel, she recently published *The Trolley Guide to Sanibel and Captiva Islands,* a local history and environmental book. Her step-grandmother died with Alzheimer's disease when in her eighties.

QUIET TIME
Deloris Selinsky

Six p. m. on Sunday
was Quiet Time at grandmama's.
Sitting in her rocking chair,
near the radio, with ear close
to the speaker, she'd listen
attentively.

I well knew, she was not
to be disturbed for anything,
except dire emergency;
and she emphasized, where I was
concerned, there was really
none of those.

Her religious program,
with Polish priest for one-half hour
sermonizing in their private language,
had grandmama in heaven's glory.
And me, hoping everything about
would be able to keep still,
long enough so as not to feel
the incriminating eyes of grandmama
glaring back at me.

DELORIS SELINSKY of Shavertown, Pennsylvania, is contest chairman and a trustee in the Pennsylvania Poetry Society. She has three poetry chapbooks published: *Thoughts in Shadow* (Jessee Poet Publications), *Reflections on a Lopsided World* (Lighthouse Enterprises) and *Fragments of Yesterday and Now–A Long Poem* (TELSTAR Publishing).

SOMETHING TO HOLD
Donna D. Vitucci

My sister and I spend rainy afternoons playing dress-up with grandma's cast off clothes and jewelry. We brush our hair and try on her discarded crystal and cameo earrings. As gypsies, Denise and I wear bathrobes with grandma's rich floral scarves tied around our waists. Her dangly earrings hang to our shoulders. The tiny space between the wall and the headboards of our two canopy beds is our cell in Russia. Poor and in prison, we ready for our escape. I pilfer slices of Velveeta cheese and Rubel's rye bread from the kitchen. We eat the crusts off the bread and put the soft insides between the pages of the fat telephone book. Then we sit on the book until the rye bread is smashed as thin as the hosts for Communion. This peasant food will keep us alive during our escape to freedom.

We visit grandma every Saturday. She wears a black flowered house dress protected by a red apron when she cooks big spaghetti dinners. Whole bay leaves float in her thick sauce. She never sits down at Christmas and Easter gatherings, but waits on us, her family, always ready to heap more food on somebody's plate. She tells us we're skin and bones; she does her best to fatten us up.

At Easter dinner grandma's walnut table with the clawed feet overflows with food. My plate holds one slice of turkey, four green olives, and a carrot stick. I don't get past grandma.

"You don't eat enough to keep a bird alive," she warns, shaking her head.

I'm embarrassed and cornered, a picky eater. Grandma holds an opposite view. "Eat. Eat well, eat some more." She lives by these words, and she spoons Italian green beans and a creamy glob of potato salad in the bare spots of my plate. I don't dare object but walk sheepishly back to my place next to Denise. Later, when grandma busies herself at the stove, mom quickly scrapes my unwanted food onto her own plate. I feel bad deceiving grandma, but her stubborn streak pays no heed to our objections.

Grandma reminds me of roses. Beautiful rose bushes line the edges of her backyard. One Easter she dances with a rose between her teeth, banging an aluminum pie plate for a tambourine. Grandma's cheeks, when we kiss them, are soft and a little damp like the inside of rose petals. She handles the perfume bottle with abandon, and the air around her holds her wonderful fragrance. For Mother's Day or her birthday we always know what to give grandma. Upon opening another gift of perfume, she exclaims gleefully, "Oh, some more of that smelly stuff." She promptly baptizes herself with the new scent, sprinkling all of us around her. Grandma's arms scoop us to her for thank you hugs and lipstick-smeared kisses. Her soft powdered cheek brushes ours and we can hardly breathe for the perfume.

Grandma's most wondrous possession is a china baby doll named Mary Ann. She sometimes let me hold her. The doll has one crack in her precious head. Grandma places her ever so delicately into my thin waiting arms just as if Mary Ann were a real baby. Her hand cups protectively beneath the injured head even after Mary Ann rests safely against my flat chest. I touch my cheek to the cool porcelain of her bald head. Her baby curls are painted on like a tight fitting cap of curlicues. She sleeps in my arms. Her eyelashes spread in two thick half moons. When I sit her up, her eyelids roll back in her head and her glassy eyes pop open, a brown greeting flecked with gold. She can't cry or drink or wet or walk or even move her head back and forth. I love her for her old-fashioned simplicity, for her beautiful baby blue dress with its fine Italian lace, and her matching bonnet. It discreetly covers the crack in her skull.

When I am seven, grandma emerges from the kitchen one Saturday afternoon and takes me aside as she wipes her hands on her red apron.

"Come in here a minute, Karen."

I follow her down the short hall. The afternoon sun filters through the sheer curtains and throws blocks of light across the floor in grandma's room. It colors the wood a gold brown like honey. The floral wallpaper grows a garden backdrop for the bouquet of perfume bottles displayed on grandma's dresser. Their scents mingle in the closed room. Mary Ann sits on a trunk nearby, her delicate dress fanned out in a wide circle of lace. Only the tips of her booties peek from beneath the tatted hem.

From the top dresser drawer grandma lifts a package and hands it to me. I glimpse pale silk before she slides the drawer closed.

"I want you to have these so you can use them tomorrow. It's a very special day, you know."

I sit on the bed to unwrap the gift. Inside are a First Communion missal and rosary. The prayer book isn't much longer than my hand. On the creamy cover Jesus points to the sacred heart glowing in His chest. I thumb quickly through the colorful pictures of miracles performed for Sunday gospels. What I find most enchanting still lies in the box, a rosary of silver and solid blue beads curled in the corner. The blue is the shade the Blessed Virgin wears in her holy card pictures. I love the round smoothness of the beads as I move each one through my fingers.

"Oh, thank you, grandma."

She sits next to me on the bed and I put my arms around her neck for a hug. Her curly black hair tickles my face. In her hair I smell aromas from her hours spent cooking in the kitchen. They mix with her perfume of the day. I breathe them in and move my head under her chin. She hugs me to her breast then pats my back as I let go of her soft, rounded shoulders.

"Now, how would you like some dinner?"

As grandma makes her way back to the kitchen, I run to the living room to show Denise my new treasures.

We retreat to grandma's basement steps where we can privately study my gifts in great detail. A paisley runner carpets the middle of each step, but if we sit off to the sides, we feel a delicious cold from the steps on our legs. Grandma's house wraps around us with the warmth of four different pots always boiling on the stove. The windows fog with condensation from the inside. We draw hearts with our initials on the steamy windowpanes that are at ground level and look in on the top basement steps. Grandma, alert to the possible danger of children playing on steps, cuts our game short.

"Get down from there. You'll fall and crack your head open."

I think of Mary Ann with the crack zigzagging through her painted curls. Her head was cool just like the basement steps.

❖❖❖

Hospital air holds artificial coolness like a refrigerator. Grandma sits in a hospital bed with the sheet pulled up to her waist. She is still. The commotion that follows her, that she usually creates, slows here to an unanswered quiet. I am twelve; I know every story will end somewhere.

We sit in her linoleum and metal room. Dad slants the blinds to filter the hot summer evening. Here grandma is not in control. She complains nurses and interns fuss over her too much. Fussing is grandma's job; it's her specialty.

Lawrence Welk conducts bubble music on the television and we pretend to watch. Grandma, in a pink nightgown, wears very red lipstick and too much rouge. I see where she dusted the face powder and where she missed. She smells of roses, or maybe all the red and pink only suggest the fragrance. When I kiss her cheek good-bye it feels soft and moist. She pulls me to her for a hug and her arthritic fingers clutch cold on my tanned arm. I think of smooth basement steps and Mary Ann's porcelain head. When I pull back from her embrace, I half expect to see a zigzag running from grandma's hairline into her black and gray curls. But it's only the makeup unevenly applied along her hairline.

❖❖❖

On the top floor of our old two-story, summer heat thickens the air long past sundown. We grow accustomed to sweating out the nights as well as the days. Unable to sleep, I wander from my bedroom. Mom stands in the hallway. She sees my short hair stuck out in sweaty tufts. I have grown too big for last summer's baby doll pajamas. She begins to reach out toward the limp eyelet at my neck. Then she reconsiders, retreats, and says, "I'll get the sheet."

She shakes out a clean sheet, snapping it in the air with a flick of her wrists. The wave floats down to the scratchy carpet. She pushes the cocktail table flush against the couch to leave one big square for our two sweaty bodies. We settle down hopefully to catch a breeze through the two front windows. Outside the crickets drone. Their familiar night whistle, that monotonous song, hypnotizes us into fuzzy sleep.

A telephone ring jars the night. I catch my breath twice—once in my dream and again when I awake and remember why uneasiness curls in my stomach. Next to me mom hiccoughs a half moan on her way to consciousness. She shivers. Her body echoes the ringing telephone.

When dad's voice answers low, mom stands at the kitchen entrance. He hugs mom and pats her back as she cries. A car speeds down the street, probably some teenagers hill hopping. Headlights shine through the front windows and swirl around the room. Every dark corner is illumined for one pearly second. In that moment of revolving light I have the impression my parents are slow dancing under one of those reflective balls you see suspended from the ceiling at New Year's Eve parties.

I watch them embrace in the hall light from my position on the sheet. Something comes loose inside me. I concentrate on taking breath after breath, to keep from falling into empty space. This tenderness of my parents opens a gulf between the normal and the unusual. I don't dare lean too close to its edge.

"I knew it. I just knew it when that phone rang," mom sobs. She wipes her eyes with her fingers.

They embrace, and dad stares over her shoulder in my direction. I lower my eyelids and alter the scene. With a half squint through my eyelashes, my parents' forms blend into edgeless shadow and the hallway bulb throws off shards of light like the Star of Bethlehem. Mom says to me, "Grandma's had another heart attack." Her voice breaks before she can finish.

I don't speak. I don't move. Tears run from the corners of my eyes, down into my ears. I feel I am drowning.

❖❖❖

The sky rolls one continuous gray. Humidity stands close, and we can't help but perspire as we dress for grandma's funeral. We keep looking, hoping for a thunderstorm out of the west. The sky opens up on the way to the cemetery, drizzling rain on the funeral procession.

Dad stares straight ahead and turns the wipers on and off as he brakes repeatedly. A silent humidity builds up in the car. We are all holding something back. Mom sticks her head out the window and assesses the weather situation.

"Now maybe we'll get some relief."

But the light rain is inconsistent and evaporates before it hits the ground.

The wake is held in grandma's basement. Grandpa has both doors open wide. Two annoying fans whir, but they don't offer much relief.

Grandma's walnut table with the clawed feet overflows with food. The smooth wood legs round up from the floor with their grasping that stops in mid-curve. I think of grandma's fingers clutching stiff on my arm that last hospital night. Someone has stacked bread and rolls near the table edge. Cakes and pies line a nearby buffet so neatly it looks like a bake sale. I wonder who brought all the food. Grandpa stirs a huge soup pot of spaghetti and dad squeezes between him and the liquor table to assume his bartender role. He ties grandma's red apron around his waist. It barely reaches.

"How about a drink, honey? Want something to eat?"

I shrug my shoulders. "I don't know."

Dad chips ice chunks and pours them into a bucket.

"Have a bite. It's good. There's plenty there."

He motions his arm towards all the food. Grandma would be pleased. Someone will make me eat.

For a while I sit on the basement steps. The coolness of the stairs seeps through my stockings. They are my first pair, but instead of making me feel grown up, they just itch. I climb upstairs to the bathroom and take them off. Voices from the basement hum reassuring background noise through the heat registers in the floor. I come out of the bathroom. Grandma's bedroom door is ajar.

Although the day is gray, her room glows with the mums and geraniums, with the soft pinks and corals in the wallpaper. I sit on the rose-colored bedspread and rub my fingers back and forth across the bumps of chenille. On the dresser the perfume bottles stand in random order. I walk over and lift the stopper out of the smallest bottle labeled "My Sin." I hold it under my nose and inhale deeply. The scent fills the back of my throat, forcing me to swallow. I squint, and through my watery eyelashes the dresser top transforms into crystal and color and light, all wavering in a prism.

I remember grandma on my First Communion Day. Dressed in a suit of some nubby material, she wears a corsage of tiny pink rosebuds pinned to her lapel. When she gives me my First Communion card with two silver dollars inside, I hug her tightly. We smash the rosebuds between us. I smell the perfume at her neck and in her hair. It is the same.

One by one I open the perfume bottles and lift the stoppers to smell each scent. Here is my grandma every Christmas and Easter and special occasion. After I open them all, I rearrange the dresser top. The old, nearly empty bottles that leak sticky perfume around the lids, I put to the back. The fuller bottles, some that have never been opened, I arrange in a front line. Amber and icy green shine through clear and frosted glass. I pick up a milky pink bottle and put its coolness to my forehead. Mary Ann watches me from the trunk beside the closet. Her gold brown eyes open that warm space I had been afraid of falling into.

I cross the room and lightly pass my fingers over her painted curls, her thick eyelashes, the crack beneath her edge of bonnet lace. I hold her and pat her back with soothing, repetitive strokes. Mary Ann's dress is splotched dark blue. Her head rests under my chin while tears roll down her porcelain cheeks.

DONNA D. VITUCCI has had poetry, fiction and articles appear in local and national publications such as *America, Bylines* and *Clifton*. She is a member of the *Ambergris* editorial staff and lives in Cincinnati, Ohio, where she strives for the perfect balance of time devoted to her two school-age sons and to freelance writing.

PORTRAIT OF ELVIRA
Lynn Buck

Sturdy large-boned woman
clad in checkered gingham
and faded blue sunbonnet,
strong hands grasping the hoe
that chops away any weeds daring
to grow in her well-tended garden,
grandmother pauses amid rows
of silk-tasseled corn and smiles at me,
her adoring young shadow.
Time overlapping ...bordered
by lacy ferns and blue hydrangeas,
standing before small white cottage,
her ample frame regal
in soft-pleated dark silk,
ash-gray hair pulled back from her face,
that kindly face of crinkled antique linen,
dimming eyes of cornflower blue peering
through rimless spectacles,
she leans on her gold-headed cane,
smiling through layers of years,
still smiling at me,
scrappy remnant of the family fabric,
searching through words and memories
for strands that interweave us

In the unsteady scrawl of an aging hand
she recorded vivid recollections
of covered wagons and log cabins,
of wool carding and soap making,
of farmers, hunters, and Civil War soldiers,
of festive Fourth of July picnics,
of her deep kinship
with rugged Ozark woodlands. Still echoing
in spring-fed streams rippling
over velvet-mossed rocks,
her voice reverberates
across yesterday's pastures

along the rick-rack of split-rail fences,
vibrations of that hearty laughter resounding
against massive granite boulders
and jagged surfaces of old Iron Mountain, echoing
her tranquil strength.
With death a looming shadow, she wrote:
"At my age I find myself traveling
over paths that wander
up and down the hills of my life...
I wade in the little creek.
I go to the green rock spring and drink
from the old gourd...
and walk among the pine trees."

The luminous energy of her words
sparks in me a current
connecting us across the borders of time.

LYNN BUCK of Hampton Bays, New York, is Missourian by birth and disposition. Her work has appeared in many national journals and anthologies including *Poets for Africa* and *The Tie that Binds*. She has published a volume of poems, *Autumn Fires*, and has completed a novel tentatively titled *Antiques Are Rarely Perfect*.

TWO WOMEN
Rhoda Gersten

Old photos of ancestors line the hall walls
going down step by step into the basement.
One, my grandmother, a young girl in Russia
looking exactly as I did at that age, at fourteen.
She was a quiet, sort of heavy old lady
and everyone said I looked just like her.
How could I look like her? She was old and pale
and wore her long, thin hair in a bun.
Flat shoes always so her feet wouldn't hurt
as she walked the New York pavements
looking for bargains—bruised oranges,
spotted bananas, still edible but cheap,
to make the food money go further.
Grandma was a calm widow, keeping house
for her two unmarried children, who supported her.
How come they all said I looked like her?
I would be wearing lipstick next year
and be allowed to pluck my eyebrows thin
like Jean Harlow's. My hair was short and curly,
in the latest style—a feather cut. And I was thin,
slim, I said to myself, not skinny.
I made my own leotards so they'd cling to my body
tighter than any you could buy,
and I hung around the dance studios
in all my spare time, not just for my classes
but to watch the grown-up goings-on of the real dancers,
especially the men, with each other.
My grandma wore loose, comfortable old dresses
and didn't know anything about such goings-on.
All she did was clean and shop and cook and pray.
She had a Hebrew blessing for everything.
Her biggest pleasure was going to the synagogue.
I couldn't figure that out. A synagogue wasn't half,
not a tenth as much fun as a dance studio.

Grandma died before I finished high school.
I don't miss her as much as I might.
I just have to look in the mirror
and there I see my grandma.

RHODA GERSTEN of Denver, Colorado, has been a modern dancer, college dance instructor, choreographer and dance therapist, and was a closet poet all that time. Now retired from dance and out of the closet, she writes in many forms and performs poetry professionally. Married fifty years, she is a mother of five and grandmother of ten.

NANA
Pamela Powell

Waiting. I gorge myself on the childhood fruit. Nana in the backyard scans the blackberries like an eagle. Bent over back, crooked, she yells scat at the cat from next door that we wanted as a kitten. Fed milk to it in the attic; it cried all night, until one day we came home and no cat cried. Nana had taken him next door to the hated neighbors. Not ours anymore. The house, too, was never ours. The silent antiques, the clock that ticked. Television on in the afternoon when I walked home from school for lunch, my heart speeding up imagining that *that* day he'd be there to greet me. Cling peaches in a can. Nana liked the soaps—well only—*Days of our Lives*— I learned to like it too. Got hooked when the baby was kidnapped and that man Marty lost his memory.

My grandmother's dress flapped in the wind. Thin cotton, bought at a rummage sale. One afternoon she fell on the hill picking blackberries. Late afternoon and she lay there until my mother came home. I was away at summer camp I guess or somewhere. The back hill is where I liked to go to escape. The swing there that went out over the hill and the fairies who lived in the trunks of trees. I knew which ones. The cliff my brother and I climbed up and down pretending it was a mountain. Wisteria purple like grapes clung there in the summer.

She was sixty-one when we moved in that summer. I don't think she wanted us to be there. The patio wasn't bricked over yet and it was before the magnolia tree split in an ice storm. I used to collect the magnolia petals and make beds for my tiny dolls, or cups and saucers for me and the bigger ones. The color of plum or jelly on a shelf when the sun shines through. Inside of the petals strange bumps and protrusions. Nana in the yard hosing the house down.

That summer my mother painted the dining room floor and it didn't dry in the heat. We had to walk outside the house to get upstairs. Nana reminds me now how she used to carry my brother, the baby, around the back with an umbrella when it rained.

She didn't want us. The parlor she once had—French china and white curtains with soft fluffy balls attached all around the edges—had to be put away. With us, the children, it wasn't safe. It became our playroom. Blocks and a dollhouse. Nana dressed me in an old-fashioned dress so my mother could take my picture with nana's antique dolls. The dolls were not to be played with; the dress was too tight and pinched my shoulders.

What did she want—nana—once she set the back hill on fire, burning off the old grass to get to new? The blackberries got thicker and thicker. Nana's dresses had more patches. She was always sewing sheets together to make them last, or to make them long enough so they'd stay tucked in.

Clothes hung outside to dry on the clothesline that turned and creaked. Nana threw hot water at any stray cats, hung pie plates out and spread netting over the berries to keep the birds away.

At night she would sit at the kitchen table picking thorns out of her arms: blackberry thorns can work their way inward. She'd show me sometimes in the dead of winter a small bluish mark deep inside her skin. She dug at them sometimes with a needle.

The blackberries smelled heady. Nights they were ripe and hung heavy over the wall where I walked barefoot on the damp walk, avoiding the thick and heavy slugs that appeared in the summer. Everything was still and stars shone between the blackberry leaves. Sometimes I picked and ate the fruit as fast as I could, hardly tasting or chewing, just gorging on the big black berries. Even the underside of the leaves scratched a little and the thorns hurt like knives.

The kitchen stove was enamel and nana made pots of iced tea. She boiled my brother's socks to get them clean. The old round washing machine in the back hall clunked and whirred. Nana was always getting something clean.

What did she want—she admired the houses on Belmont Hill. When she drove me home from piano lessons sometimes she'd make me get out and ask the people questions about their house or garden. Strangers—she'd stop and ask how much the house had sold for or what kind of shrub they had in their garden. I wasn't allowed to say no. She used to sell real estate. She liked the old neat and tidy houses best, the ones that showed no sign of children.

But she loved us too. And was proud of our accomplishments. I could hear nana tell her friend Florence on the phone. We never did anything right to suit her, but she taught us. How to pack china in boxes. How to store clothes in mothballs for the summer. How to tie a box on the edge to get it really tight.

But nothing was ours there in that house. I was always wanting. The doll clothes I'd found in a box in my closet but wasn't allowed to have. They were too good for me. I might lose them.

Nana, I see you lying out in the blackberries. The day you fell and broke your leg. A cricket jumped over your head, one leg crooked at an unnatural angle. The rocky bank. Blackberries staining your dress. That pale blue and green one with the snaps down the front and pockets, and your legs thick and swollen, though not so swollen as they are now. And your skin so white, almost creamy.

You're lying so still there and you don't get up. In a way I'm glad and I picture that fire you set—the flames leaping up among golden grasses—and it's hot and it's flickering and the sun and all of it moves to consume you.

Later I was hungry and the berries hung there cool and juicy in the shade. Globules like clusters of grapes in the cold of autumn. Morning when the dew sits just so and toes are cold in the damp grass. I cry for my mother who's carrying nana down the hill. But now my eyes aren't teary. I have no way to cry. Nana is still and the spiders come and dance about and make webs.

She never went to the sea with us. Had she ever been to the sea? We brought home sand, in our suits, on our skin. Nana complained how the kitchen floor was gritty. "You brought the beach home with you," she'd snap.

I wonder if she knew how blue the water was there, how the sand sparkled and you could climb for miles on the rocks at the end of Singing Beach. We ate sandwiches that sometimes she made. The sea our escape.

Nana set the hill on fire when we weren't there. Came home to fire engines wailing. That sharp sound that goes in through the blood.

We were unpacking boxes in the attic to see what was there. "Your mother got rid of all that good furniture. She never thinks. She's never home to do anything."

Now nana's eyesight is failing. She's too blind to see what's in the boxes, has to be told, reminded, what's wrapped in paper. She doesn't see the dust settling in the hall, on the legs of the chairs. The places I used to dust so carefully to please her. Now nana doesn't know how dirty the kitchen floor is. How hairs from my brother's dog blow across the floor in clumps like milkweed, how the dust on the refrigerator is so thick. She doesn't see what she's eating on her plate—and doesn't know that when I'm there I clean, wipe down the counters, dust the dining room, rewash the dishes she's put away dirty—but only when she's not looking. If she knows I'm cleaning she will tell me I'm doing it wrong. Using too much hot water or the wrong soap. Or a rag she's been saving for something else.

When I am there I wander through the house like a lost child. Staring at the pictures of me, my brother, and sister growing up. Frozen children with smiles perched in trees, or on the steps in a row on the back hill. Some of the pictures have faded and we are beginning to look like ghosts. Like we were never really here at all.

Nana is smaller now. She gets to her bed at the end of the house with a walker. The room that used to be the parlor, and then the playroom, and is now a room for storage and for her to sleep. It is as if she is being put in storage too.

I read to her, "Just a little from the headlines," she says and she listens hard to every word. I see her mind working, like a steel trap, and remember that someone once said nana would have made a good dictator.

I help her pull off the tight support hose over her swollen ankles, and swing her legs up onto the bed. A light breeze comes in through the windows where the magnolia tree once stood. It is hot; it is summer. The leaves of the Japanese maple rustle against the screen. Nana's legs look so pretty there, all of her in a curve like a comma in an old slip she wears for the hot weather.

Everything is crowded in around her. The big desk. The toy cupboard. The winter clothes my sister is storing here. Now it is safe to throw things away in the wastebaskets because nana can't see. But then you couldn't; anything thrown away was likely to be fished back out again and could resurface anywhere. Socks we considered beyond darning were too good for rags and were put away in boxes marked mending in the sprawling curve of nana's pen.

Blackberry. The fruit can be so sour. I remember my mother went away to New Mexico. I thought she might not come back. After all he didn't come back though I waited and waited. Expected he'd show up some afternoon on Pleasant Street, pick me up in his arms and away we'd go. I don't know what I thought would happen after that.

Nana told me things about daddy I didn't want to hear. How he borrowed money from her for cases of champagne and never paid her back. How he was so stubborn, and we, the children, were like him. "You're stubborn just like your father," she'd say—as if we had no choice about it. We were stuck with his stubbornness; it was in our blood. And if he was crazy that must be in our blood too. Blood the blackberry thorns draw up to the surface. Tiny red balls of blood welling up from a scratch or tear. Sometimes it felt good to walk through the bushes. To feel the thorns tear at skin. To feel anything real.

My room had a lock on the door. There was safety in having a lock on the door. They couldn't get in.

Underneath the bed alligators hid and it was one long leap to get there from the doorway. At night the rain fell in a heavy patter, thick through the leaves. And the smell of bread my sister was baking filled the house until early in the morning when she was finished. Sometimes late at night the phone rang and it was daddy. Was he crazy or not? I didn't know. Was it him? Did he love me—he said so—was it real? I would hand the phone to my mother who had just awakened. And back in my bed curl up in a little ball.

Nana said, "I told them; they should never have gotten married. They were too young. And he was reckless, your father. Always had to make a show." Yet even now a photograph of my mother and father on their wedding day sits on nana's bureau in the upstairs hall. Now she can't see it. Does she remember it's there?

At the top of the step where the slate lies broken stands nana. Bent over she stabs the ground with the purple pitchfork from England. Bends to smell a rose and breaks off a deadhead. Her head wrapped in a rag, she's wearing some old man's raincoat, something she bought at the Armenian rummage sale when I was small.

We used to go there—she and I—and I'd squeeze in line right in front of all the old ladies who'd grumble, but wouldn't stop me. Nana pushed me there so I could be first in for the bargains. I hated being shoved to the front but took delight in knowing I had a good eye. Nana in her green plush hat—she'd come find me with blue jeans over one arm for my brother who had patches over patches on the old pairs. I would be poring over the children's books—picking out the old ones—I knew which were good—or digging in piles and piles of clothing for flannel nightgowns, jackets, sweaters for ten cents that were good as new. I would bring things to nana for her approval—something I thought we needed—and most of the time she'd agree and buy it.

The dusty smell of church basements, so familiar. The old women in black muttering in Armenian, sharp elbows and big bosoms. The embarrassment of being made to try on something between racks of old coats and prom dresses when nana said, "No one will see."

We went to church fairs together, never paying too much for a pair of wool mittens. Nana would find someone she'd sold a house to twenty years earlier and stand talking forever. Sometimes I'd get dizzy standing there with the bundles.

Once we went to a doll auction and nana made me sit on my hands. She bid on a box for $5.00. You didn't know what you'd get; the table was too far away. I sat next to nana on the hard folding chairs praying she'd bid on the bisque baby doll I'd showed her. Life-size, like a real baby. I watched the auctioneer lift it to the stand. I could feel it cradled in my arms; it even had a dent in the head like a fontanel. I tried to look eager and as if I deserved it all at the same time, but nana didn't budge. The numbers got higher and I couldn't breathe. Nana didn't move. I wanted to wink at the auctioneer, or raise one eyebrow, but I didn't know how. I could pay if I sold enough boxes of Campfire Girl candy. Three hundred and fifty...the auctioneer paused...sold. A man came and took the baby away.

Later we picked up the box of stuff nana had bought. She wasn't pleased, said, "It was my granddaughter who raised her hand to bid—she didn't know what she was doing. I don't want this junk." They let her return it. I was relieved. In the box a gaudy Jack-in-the-box leaned over to one side, sluggish. Behind the counter I saw the baby doll waiting to be claimed.

PAMELA POWELL recently completed a year teaching English as a Second Language in a Prague *gymnasium*. Prior to that she taught sailing for Outward Bound on the eastern seaboard, having worked on boats for two years in the Caribbean. Her children's novel set in the West Indies will be published by Viking (Penguin) Press in 1992.

THE BRAID
Cheryl Marie Wade

gramma's hands
were big and doughy and restless
they crocheted a garden on muslin for my bed
brewed strong black tea
shuffled the deck for solitaire

an old woman's hands

but once they had been pale and light
and held a tortoise shell brush
once they held a tortoise shell brush
while she sat before a mirror
brushing her long wheat hair
her thick wheat hair that I knew only gray
except in the braid she wove from her brush leavings
the braid she gave to me so I would always remember—

before the ten pregnancies
and five miscarriages
before the four children she raised
and the daughter who disappeared
before the five grandchildren
and the great-grandchildren
before

she was a woman

wheat colored

CHERYL MARIE WADE of Berkeley, California, has been writing and performing professionally for six years. She edits a semi-annual anthology of disability arts for Squeaky Wheels Press. Her work appears frequently in small press journals and anthologies and is forthcoming in *Ms* and in the Seal Press collection, *She Who was Lost is Remembered: Healing from Incest through Creativity.*

I KNEW MY GRANDMA
Mary Sewall-Hebert

I knew my grandma, only as old,
a woman worn by sorrows untold.
I never saw her younger years—
her secret hopes, private fears.

To me she seemed so hard and brittle;
adults are gods, when one is little.
I cringed in awe when she would scold.
I knew her anger only as old.

But who was she when just a bride?
Or as a young mother whose newborns died?
Ten times she gave the gift of birth;
the crib for three, a graveyard's earth.

When one year wed, her firstborn was lost
Was that the price that love would cost?
Two others her arms would never enfold
so the living knew her bosom as cold.

Once young as I, she must have known
youth's joy before her heart turned stone.
The aching loss of grief unconsoled—
I knew my grandma, only as old.

MARY SEWALL-HEBERT is a folk artist specializing in dolls which she sells at craft fairs throughout northern Wisconsin, where she lives with her husband and three sons. Currently, her muse is silent, but her work has appeared in many small presses, and she plans to publish four books of poetry.

OVER THE RIVER AND THROUGH THE WOODS
Nancy Mathews

To make the time pass faster, we sang, "Over the river and through the woods to grandmother's house we go," as mother, father and I drove the seventy miles to my grandmother's house. I did not love my only living grandmother. I did love the countryside where she lived and happily spent every summer in one of Grandmother Brown's summer houses, which we rented. But if grandmother invited me to stay with her when my parents returned to Richmond, I politely refused because I was afraid of her sharp-eyed judgment of me.

I had my own judgment of Emily Ridenhour Brown, who was my father's mother. I saw her as a stern, cold, straight-backed woman with her long gray hair pulled tightly into a bun at the nape of her neck. She wore home-made calico dresses with prim white collars, pinned, on special occasions, with an inexpensive brooch.

My feelings for Grandmother Brown were mixed with anxiety and respect. Mother had no doubt influenced me with stories of her early married life in the country, after World War I. She, a city girl, and father, a country boy, were forced to live in a platform tent, in the orchard with the geese and chickens, because grandmother had filled the large house with paying boarders. Mother did not show much affection for her mother-in-law and consequently neither did I. She did admire grandmother's pioneer heritage (my ten-year-old great-grandmother had come to California by covered wagon in 1851.) Living off the land since childhood had formed grandmother into a hard-working widow, who managed, with the help of her two unmarried daughters, a summer resort, country store and post office. I was in awe of how hard she worked; she rarely left home because, as she would say, "How would the girls get along without me?" Grandmother worked from sunup to sundown. When she wasn't running the resort, she gardened and canned and cooked. She thought I was lazy; in her time, children were born to work, but I refused to crawl around on my hands and knees picking up prunes with the other summer kids. I was an embarrassment to the hard working Brown family.

Grandmother and I had nothing in common except my father. He didn't talk to me about her and I never saw her show affection toward her five children. But every time I put on my bathing suit, she would stop me on the way to the river with the warning, "Don't step in a hole. Be careful, Nancy Mae, or you'll drown." And I knew that in her heart she cared about me. One summer afternoon, sitting on the back porch steps, she let me comb out her clean, fine white hair while she dried it in the sun. That is my only memory of touching her and I felt privileged.

We sometimes ate Sunday dinner together. I can see grandmother jumping up from the table to fetch whatever she imagined we needed. Mother would give me the eye that said, "Get up and get it. Don't let your grandmother wait on you." I was saying to myself, "What's the rush? I don't even want that glass of milk." She moved quickly for an old lady and I was not at all interested in keeping up with her.

Sometimes I helped her with the chores. I wish I had asked about her early life and my father's childhood, but I never realized that it would become important to me. We gathered eggs from the nesting boxes and I watched her wring the White Leghorns' necks before plunging them into boiling water. I was fascinated with the process but did not enjoy the chicken fricassee which appeared on my plate at dinner. When we spent time together, she didn't have much to say, whereas I talked non-stop until she said, "That's enough, Nancy Mae."

When grandmother died at eighty-two, I was fourteen. Mother ruled that I was too young to go to the funeral; I guess she wanted to protect me from what she saw as the pain of death and the embarrassment of mourning. I couldn't tell what my father or anyone else felt about my grandmother's death, but I felt like an outsider. I, a lonely only child, stayed by myself at grandmother's house on the day of her funeral and wondered if anyone had ever gotten to know her.

NANCY MATHEWS of Sebastopol, California is a third generation Californian and is presently writing *Growing Up in California*. She has had several poems published, the latest in the Russian River Writers' Guild Anthology, *A Stone's Throw*. Her essay also appears in *Women of the 14th Moon* (The Crossing Press, 1991).

A CAUTIONARY TALE
Carol Biederman

To me my grandfather was no more than a faded sepia photograph, a stern man posed against the masts and rigging of the clipper ships he had sailed. But grandma was alive, with quick, black eyes that snapped with energy and spirit, swift fingers that kneaded and mended, a long black skirt that swirled around her ankles as she walked.

On mild Seattle afternoons we worked in the garden or picked blackberries to can. When it rained, we baked, or read, or cut paper dolls from the Sears catalogue, making large families on the dining room table.

Of course, we never played paper dolls or did anything else in the afternoon until grandma had finished "resting" her eyes. To do this, she retired to her room and sat in her rocking chair. After a suitable amount of time, she would come out, or, if I had been especially good, she would invite me in to look at her collections. One of these consisted of silver spoons. The spoons were from all over the world, and I imagined that my grandfather had brought them to her from his ports-of-call. They were carefully stored in tiny pockets stitched in a dark red flannel cloth. Each spoon had its own pocket, and when they were all in place, grandma would fold over the edges of the red flannel, roll it up, and tie it tightly to keep the spoons from tarnishing.

Another of grandma's collections consisted of buttons. Some were tiny with pictures painted on them: a house, a flower, a tiny animal. Others were big and glittered with rhinestones and pearls. She had a story about each dress from which the buttons had come. "I wore this dress when I married your grandfather." Or, "This was the dress I wore to your Uncle Frank's christening." Or, "I took this dress when the boys and I sailed with your grandfather to Hawaii."

And singly, her vial of gall stones. How gently I held it, tipping it, watching the amber fluid inside sweep the tiny particles from the bottom to the top, from the top back to the bottom.

"Stones," my grandma would say. "Stones, from in here." She would point vaguely to her midsection. "They had to cut them out." She would rock back and forth, nodding her head, yes. Yes, the rocker would agree.

And I would shiver with delicious fright, imagining grandma's belly with its long knife cut across it.

When we had company, the guests slept in my room, and I would sleep in the big bed with grandma. When she got undressed, she would tell me not to look but I always peeked. She would pull her flannel nighty down and undress under it, but I caught glimpses of her body with its wrinkled flesh, her tiny, brownnippled breasts, her belly with its little folds of skin. Now, I wondered, how does it look with its knife cut?

"Here," she would point again to her belly and then look back at the vial in my hands.

I handled it carefully, fearful that I might break it, and the stones would escape across our lives again. How well I remembered the dreadful morning when daddy ran to the bathroom door crying, "You okay, ma?" But she wasn't okay, and the doctor came. He examined grandma, and then he and daddy drove her to the hospital. We made many trips to visit her, but they wouldn't let little girls in, because little girls carried germs. Or so they told me. I sat alone in the lobby of the hospital and waited for mama and daddy to come down from grandma's room.

When grandma came home from the hospital, her hair, which she had so carefully kept dyed black, grew out white. She lay in her big bed with her hands limp on the white spread. I sat, sadly, and stroked her hands saying, "Poor grandma." It seemed a long time before she was up and able to play with me again.

No, I wouldn't risk dropping the vial, wouldn't risk a spill, wouldn't risk unleashing the stones.

"Stones," she would say. "Dirt in my stomach." The rocker would stop, and she would lean forward, her face close to mine, her black eyes intent.

"Wash your food carefully, child. Very carefully."

Then she would lean back and rock, nodding her wisdom to the squeak of the chair.

CAROL BIEDERMAN of Sonoma, California, is a retired elementary school teacher who enjoys writing poetry and prose. An only child, she has written a collection of short stories about her favorite playmate, her grandmother, which she has entitled *The Other Child in the House. A Cautionary Tale* is from that collection.

BITTERSWEET
Mary M. Harris

I.

I envied my friends their grandmothers,
apple-cheeked dumplings with bosoms
smelling of vanilla and talcum powder.
Mine was lanky and stiff as a scarecrow.
She wore self-pity like an apron
and dispensed love like postage stamps.

Her blood could not process sugar.
Disease consumed her, injected
bitterness into every conversation.
Each holiday she swore would be her last.
What she couldn't control obsessed her.
I turned callous to her biting wit,
letters written with venom, words
barbed like a cactus. Her veins
collapsed like blasted mines.
Still, it took half a century
for her to die.

II.

In her eighties,
sometimes the mask slipped.
Unguarded, she retrieved memories
from a vault, stopped
mid-speech to appraise me,
not with her critical crow's eye
but amazed, revealing images of me
as a newborn first opening my eyes
or a toddler standing in a booth
at some long-ago restaurant.
Reliving those moments when
it took so little to win her love,
I forgave her everything.

MARY M. HARRIS was named after her maternal grandmother, Mary Margaret
Gleason. She never knew her father's mother who lived in Czechoslovakia. MARY M.
HARRIS writes poetry, fiction and nonfiction. Her work has appeared in over forty
publications. She lives in Simi Valley, California, with her twelve-year-old son, George.

PAPER WHITE FACES
Judith Strickert Montoya

The bespectacled girl
climbed climbed
the steep wooden
steps of her grandmother's
stalwart German mein

willed her cheek
to accept a kiss
from the blanched lips
carved in granite by the
childhood sculptor of oppression

felt...the pewter eyes

> ...the impregnable shawl
> cladding an edifice
> unrelenting as the
> reels of the primitive machine
> sucking up sodden laundry and
> spitting it into washtubs
> lining the dank
> walls of her basement

> ...the stolid black
> shoes of aching
> loneliness treading
> the March snow that
> claimed her husband's heart

> ...the ticktock ticktock
> of the brass pendulum
> subtracting age-old friends

fastened on her gnarled
fingers   in and out
in and out   soundlessly
adding needle prick wounds
to crusty fingertips
and beheld
the fabric of her

and knew
the tenacity of her
endures
in the salient faces of
the paper white daffodils
ever recurring
at her granite carved name

JUDITH STRICKERT MONTOYA, a fledgling writer residing in Falls Church, Virginia, writes poetry, children's stories and articles for a cancer newsletter in the moments she captures in between keeping pace with three adolescent boys and a two-year-old, bushels of smelly athletic clothes, and her expansive perennial garden.

A FRACTION OF HER GOODNESS

LIFE LINES
Arline G. Cogan

Grandmother saved string
from bakery and butcher shop packages
and rolled it into balls
    "Never can tell when you'll need it,"
    she'd say.

Round and round
she wound the long and short strands,
her gnarled fingers shaped a smooth ball.
Intent upon her task, her face became serene.

Like the strings, she gathered
our large family and wove us together
binding sisters, brothers, children
and colonies of cousins into a tight knit clan.

Now, I covet her skill and composure
as pulled by demands of nuclear life
my self unravels into a tangled mass.

I rush to tie it up.
I need a ball of grandmother's string.

Born in Brooklyn, New York, granddaughter of Irish immigrants, ARLINE G. COGAN began writing poetry in 1978. Her poems have been published in numerous anthologies. Her first nationally published prose piece, a vignette about her grandmother, appeared in *Redbook*. ARLINE G. COGAN now lives in Desoto, Texas.

DREAMS OF YOU
Gayle Hunter Sheller

did you know when I was little
and needed to run away
it would always be to you?
you were the mother of my body,
its shape, its color—
large bones,
wide hips for spilling big babies,
red hair, clear blue eyes.
though I was born of a small
mother who feared my size,
I knew love from your strong hands,
mothering from your secret smiles,
promises from your eager eyes.
grandma of peonies
towering over my head;
grandma of hidden sweets,
offered a piece at a time,
stolen treasure;
grandma of stout, tall legs
that took the young woman you,
in skirts kicked from round your
stone solid ankles,
to the top of the Middle Sister;
grandma, your bride's day picture
on my wall, a lap of roses and
a veil of brilliance lighting
a vaguely self-conscious smile
that knows you are pretty;
grandma, I miss you to run home to,
I, who am every bit your size.
sometimes your legacy is too
heavy to carry, a heritage of
hard work, order and lush gardens.

I close my eyes and smell you,
taste your garden corn,
and know just long enough
it is okay to be me.
do you know
when I need to run away
it is to dreams of you?

GAYLE HUNTER SHELLER, blessed to know both of her grandmothers well into her adulthood, makes her home in Springfield, Oregon, with her math-teacher husband and four sons. She is active in local politics, particularly in issues dealing with the homeless. GAYLE HUNTER SHELLER writes, and she also works in a children's bookstore.

THE LEGACY
Cos Barnes

"The hour hand can be moved in either direction," the jeweler said, peering at me over the top of the magnifying glasses he wore, "but the minute hand only clockwise."

His large hands moving adroitly over the delicate mechanisms, he quietly instructed me in the care of my grandmother's 90-year-old clock which I had recently inherited. "Wind it on the same day every week," he cautioned. "In case it runs down and is not striking correctly, start it back up by turning the minute hand to 12 and allowing it to strike. If it does not strike the correct number of times, move the hour hand to whatever time it strikes, then set the clock to the correct time and give it a chance to strike."

His words of advice echoed in my head as I placed the aged timepiece in the center of my mantel and inserted the key as I had seen my grandmother do so often so many years ago. Slowly, I turned the key to the left, using the utmost care to make a complete revolution lest the spring coil back with a jolt.

"To start it, shove it gently," the watchmaker had said. "Listen to the rhythm of its tick. Your ear will tell you if it is not right."

Remembering the trust my grandmother, a woman of a devout Primitive Baptist faith, had in the accuracy of the clock, I marveled that the repairman had only had to add a new pendulum rod and suspension spring. The eight-day clock was as good as new, although it had been stored in a pantry for years.

"Granny relied on that clock," my mother told me. "If it stopped in the night, she woke up. One time the clock had ceased to run. Then suddenly, without warning, it chimed. I can see and hear granny now. 'Something has happened to Jess,' she gasped. It was months later that she received word that her son Jess had been killed in battle in France. The year was 1917."

When, in 1927, my grandmother moved with her family from the country into town, she insisted on carrying the clock on her lap. I did the same thing when I transported it from her home in Virginia to mine in North Carolina.

As I grew accustomed to the soft ticking and the reliable chiming on both the hour and the half-hour, I could feel this chronometer connecting me again to my grandmother who died thirty years ago. I could feel the clock curbing my impatience, ignoring my exasperation with interruption, soothing me into a calm acceptance of circumstances, as if it were reminding me of the qualities of perseverance, patience and piety my grandmother possessed. It now measures the rhythms of my life as it did hers. And it does so with no glaringly red digital announcement, but rather with a steady tolling, the numerals on its face obliterated by that which it measures. And as it moves at its unhurried pace, it prompts me to take my time, not to rush the present, but rather to relax and savor each day as it unfolds. It reminds me that some of my days will be resplendently happy, some will be marred by tragedy; some will result in triumphant accomplishment, others will be boring and frustrating.

And as I listen to granny's clock marking the days of my life as it did hers, I think of her.

Her legacy includes more than a clock; it includes a personal item—a nightgown. Being one of many grandchildren, I consider myself fortunate to have it.

"Would you like to have one of granny's gowns?" my aunt asked me recently when I was visiting in my hometown.

"Would I?" I answered incredulously as she opened the lid of an aged walnut cedar-lined chest and rummaged through layers of unused Christmas presents, unworn purchases, and an assortment of crocheted and embroidered items. I had no idea the gowns existed.

Drawing out several delicate handmade nightgowns—once white, now yellowed by time—she said, "Pick the one you want."

"How old are they?" I asked breathlessly as I inspected each one.

"Granny had a cousin make them years ago when her health began to fail. They have to be more than forty years old," my aunt said.

I inspected them carefully. Made of softest cotton, they featured yokes with tiny tucks and insertions of lace. The one I chose is trimmed at the neck and long sleeves with Hamburg lace. Three buttons adorn the front. The buttonholes are handworked.

"Can you imagine anyone now taking the time to work buttonholes by hand on a nightgown?" I asked as I slipped the garment over my head. It is wider than I and much shorter, but how I treasure this memento of my grandmother.

The nightgown lies in my cedar chest now. I will not wear it. I will not try to whiten it; I would never risk its fragility to bleach. I will simply save it and someday pass it on to one of my daughters.

It is not as durable as a piece of furniture, or as lasting as an earring of gold, but it is now mine, and how I cherish it. It is my tangible reminder of a woman who bore eleven children, reared six step-children as well, and still found the time and heart to serve as a mid-wife when there was need.

In my mind's eye, I see her still—sitting on the back porch peeling peaches for canning, or sitting in her chair in her bedroom, either crocheting yards of delicate trim for pillowcases, or reading her Bible. I can see the slow, circular motion she used to massage liniment into her aching, rheumatic legs.

Etched vividly in my remembrance is the way she removed the pins from the bun at the back of her head, took one of the two combs she wore on either side of it, combed her thinning hair, then took the strands of hair from the comb and tied them in a tiny bow. As youngsters, we grandchildren delighted in being the recipient of one of those bows made of strands of silver.

I see her, dressed in black, and accompanied by her kin, going to the cemetery on Armistice Day in November each year to mourn again the death of Jess.

I taste again the strawberry pie and wonder anew why my meringues lack the tiny honey-colored beads of sugar hers always possessed. I see her presiding over Christmas Day dinner when the whole clan gathered—and the children— who in those days were supposedly seen and not heard—ate at the last table.

I remember taking granny for rides on Sunday afternoons. She always rested her right hand on the door handle as if she still did not completely trust machine or driver.

And with regret I recall the teenager's exasperation at having to babysit with the one who did it so often and so willingly for me...and the declining years when her thoughts began to wander back to her childhood, and she would plead, "Get the wagon, I want to go home"... and the desolate emptiness when she was gone.

And I wonder, what did I inherit from my strong, but gentle, grandmother?

After all of the years of watching her, I cannot crochet. My cooking wins no accolades, and rearing three children nearly did me in.

I have the same short, stocky legs, the gray which, like hers, began its trespass in my hair in my twenties and achieved total dominance in my forties. But what else?

A fraction of her goodness, I pray...and her clock...and her gown.

COS BARNES of Southern Pines, North Carolina, has curtailed her writing in recent months. But with son-in-law home from Saudi Arabia, two new grandchildren added to the fold, a home addition completed, and the planning of the wedding of the third child done, she looks forward to pursuing her career.

THE BUDDHA
June Hudson

My grandmother was a Southern Baptist
but had a black plaster Buddha sitting
on the dresser in her bedroom under a
colored picture of Jesus.

Staring down at me with piercing blue eyes
like my mother's, Jesus followed me closely
wherever I walked in the room and made me
feel guilty. But Buddha's eyes were almost
closed and he let grandma and me
burn incense in his lap.

We bought boxes of incense shaped like
candy corn from the dime store,
burning one piece after another until
everything in the small farm house
soaked up the sweet smells of
sandalwood, musk and lavender rose.

When grandpa complained that even
the okra and tomatoes that we ate
every night from his garden tasted like
the incense, grandma laughed and told him
not to go spoiling our fun.

Sundays when we went to church,
grandma sat solid in the pew,
eyes half opened, lips half smiling.
Slipping my small smooth fingers under
her large calloused hands folded loosely
in her lap, I sat still, listening to
the sermon about sinning and burning
in hell. She softly squeezed my fingers
as I nuzzled closer to her firm body.

Grandma smelled sweeter than the Buddha.

Born in Dallas, Texas, JUNE HUDSON attended the University of Texas before moving
to California where she has taught art and photography. Her poetry recently won a
Jessamyn West Writing Award and has been published in *Santa Clara Review, Verve,
Tomcat* and will appear in a forthcoming *Sonoma Mandala.*

THE CHANGING EMBRACE
Colleen J. Houghtaling

It seems to me my childhood days
were filled with magic charms
when I would visit grandma and
she'd wrap me in her arms.

The sweet perfume which filled her house
was that of fresh-baked bread;
warm slices spread with home-made jam
we'd nibble while we read.

We'd laugh away the afternoons
together, shelling peas;
and I was honored when she'd share
her childhood memories.

Although I'm grown, my visits few,
I still can feel those charms
whenever I'm with grandma and
I wrap her in my arms.

COLLEEN J. HOUGHTALING grew up in Knoxville, Pennsylvania, and now lives in the country near her hometown with her husband and pets. She received a B.S. in elementary education from Mansfield University, taught as a substitute for seven years, and then worked as a reporter and editor for local newspapers. Her writing has appeared in such publications as *Grit, Byline, Ellery Queen* and *Midwest Poetry Review.* Currently she is writing a murder mystery.

COLORED PRISMS ON THE FLOOR
Meg Gagnon

Grandma Miller moved in with my family when I was five, two years after grandpa died in 1945. She was a rather small woman with sharp features. She wore funny, round glasses which she seemed to prefer down on her nose as opposed to up on her eyes. Her thin brown hair, now streaked with gray, lay in soft, tight curls and was held close to her head in a hairnet. Born back in the middle of the 19th century, she was understandably old-fashioned.

Dad left early each morning to drive to the city to work and returned late at night, tired. Mama worked long hours on the farm and my brother and sisters were in school. That left grandma and me in the house.

Grandma taught me how to care for my clothes and drawers. She taught me how to cut out quilt pieces and lay quilt tops. She gave me my first cooking lessons. She told me true stories of her family down in Ohio growing up together. She told me fables like *The Little Match Girl.* I would listen to the story of the poor little girl who went from door to door trying to sell matches in the dead of winter. And how she was found one morning frozen to death under the bushes outside a house. I would cry and then beg grandma to tell it one more time. She had a way of telling a story that completely captured my attention. Besides her teaching me skills like sewing and cooking, and entertaining me with her stories, I had a full time confidante. Grandma was my closest and best friend in early childhood.

One day, my mother was taking my sisters to a nearby town for piano lessons and I wanted to go, too. Apparently, my mother didn't know it and she drove out of the drive with me running and crying down the porch steps after her. Mama didn't hear me. She drove away and I turned back to the house heartbroken and sobbing because I was left behind.

Grandma met me at the porch door with her big Hubbard apron wrapped around her and ready for work. She never was without an apron unless she was leaving the house or it was meal time. She told me we were going to make peanut butter cookies and I could make the cross marks on top. Soon I had forgotten my tears and heartbreak and grandma and I were busy making cookies. She brought a chair up close to the kitchen counter and I climbed up, armed with a fork and completely enveloped in one of her aprons. Grandma showed me how to make the little crosses on the top of a cookie. I stood on the chair painstakingly applying the fork first one way and then the other. It wasn't long before grandma was taking cookies out of the oven to cool. When mama got home, I was so impressed with my fine artistic work on those cookies that, although I had not forgotten that she had left without me, I had at least forgiven her.

When I was about seven, grandma found out she had cancer of the liver. She read about every cure there was at the time, including the grape cure, which was a notion that if a person ate bunches and bunches of grapes, somehow the cancer would go away.

The parlor had been converted into a bedroom so that grandma would not have to go upstairs anymore. She would sit in her rocking chair cutting grapes in half, taking out the seeds and eating grape after grape. During this time she was able to get around and still help in the house. She and I spent a lot of time in the parlor with the sun streaming through the cut glass windows, making colored prisms on the floor.

In that room, grandma showed me how to cut quilt blocks and how to lay them out for a pretty pattern. She was raised in a time of poverty when the pieces used in quilts were the best part of the tail of an old shirt or the bodice of a worn dress. There might be scraps left over from the sewing, but she came from a time when getting a new dress was like our getting a new car—it only happened once every couple of years.

I would sit beside grandma on a stool by her chair, and we would trace out postcard quilt pieces, making sure that we could use every bit of good material to the best advantage. Then I, with my little scissors, and she with her big ones would cut block after block. She laid them in neat piles in a dress box where they would lie flat and we could see the different colors easily.

As we traced and cut, she would tell me about her brothers and sisters and of how they lived so poorly as children. Some of the stories she told of her mischievous brothers would make us laugh and laugh. She explained that her mother punished them by boxing their ears instead of spanking them as most children were punished. Her storytelling ability made these distant times come to life.

She spoke with pride about how she had met grandpa, her eighth grade school teacher. She had been a shy young woman who had not yet had a beau. Most of the girls had crushes on the young school teacher. It was rather a surprise to her and certainly an honor that he would notice her. He seemed to know so much more than she. He had come from a family of teachers; she had come from a family of poor dirt farmers. There was not much time in her family's life to be educated. However, grandma did complete the eighth grade. It was then that Mr. Harvey Miller came courting. Grandma's mother was very particular about whom her children chose as friends. Grandpa was an educated man and well respected in the community. Grandma said that her mother would tell neighbors of how her daughter had made such a fine catch. She described grandpa with respect for his education and knowledge, but also with a lot of love.

Despite the crates of grapes that grandma consumed, her illness did not abate and soon she was bedridden. Mama had to admit she could not care for grandma, the farm and her family. After much discussion, they decided mutually that grandma would move to a place where she could get full-time nursing and mama could have a rest. So grandma went to a house a few miles from the farm, where a lady nursed a handful of terminal patients.

Mama would take me to visit grandma and I would talk to her, now thin and barely able to speak at times. Then I would go outdoors and wait for mama. The house used to be part of a turkey farm and the big turkey cage barns were still there. I would go out and inspect them and imagine big turkeys gobbling all over.

One morning mama sat at the kitchen table looking as if she had cried all night. Grandma had died during that night. I don't remember crying, though I might have. We younger children didn't go to the funeral. For me, at least, this only meant I had no one to listen to me as much, and no one to tell me *The Little Match Girl* over again.

When I remember Grandma Miller now, my thoughts go back to that parlor and all the quilt pieces we cut. We never did complete a quilt top together. We laid many pieces out in various designs. We would pick up the pieces and put them back in the box again to be laid out another day in a new pattern. Now, years later, a quilt from those blocks covers my bed, one tangible bit of evidence of all that I shared and learned with grandma.

MEG GAGNON owns a medical transcription business which she runs from her home in Indianapolis, Indiana. She enjoys writing about her early life, studying her family's genealogy, growing flowers and vegetables, traveling, meeting new people and making new friends. Four cats share her life and her home.

A SUPERMARKET SUPPLY OF DELIGHT
Lynda Calabrese

My grandma smiles
as she sits
in her wheel chair
holding on to the joy
that has simmered for ninety-one years.

She has no recall of her voyage
when she was six
cramped in steerage like cattle
with her brothers
nauseated from Poland
to Ellis Island, New York.

Freckled hands
that fashioned feathered hats
in Manhattan haberdasheries
cling to the same old photos
of great-grandchildren that
hug her in honey-dipped dreams.

Grandma says now she's a stupid head.
In ten minutes
she'll probably forget
this long distance call.
She says at her age
you love to remember
but oh, how you hate to forget

Lena Coo forgets
she's lost her Louie.
Smells of Noxema
and cigar smoke
make him seem near.

She could be in Rockaway
Brooklyn or Miami,
Beverly Manor Nursing Home
could be anywhere.

She misses all the tumult
and laughter
as she stares at the
World Series on the community TV
Her favorite Giants play in Los Angeles
and she doesn't even know the pitcher's name.

Grandma can't remember when
the only washing machine
was at Aunt Selma's
two doors down the block
or stuffing family and tenants
into her basement
to watch the fights on Friday night
while four grandchildren slept
in houses connected by intercom.

But grandma remembers
her sky blue hydrangeas
purple peonies
the size of a grown man's two fists.
She remembers her Victory Garden's
tomatoes, string beans and strawberries
cabbage, eggplants and lettuce.

Her eyes become slits when she smiles
sandwiched between brow and chubby cheeks,
when she thinks of her crab apples
and barbeques on the lawn
when everyone she loved lived next to her.
Whoever got up first made coffee
and strangers didn't comb her hair
or make her smile.

Sometimes she thinks
she's downstairs at Forte Towers
she'll pick up some Milk of Magnesia
and the *New York Times* after her club swim.
Her Swim Chicks are getting so catty
they're starting to grow whiskers and tails.
She needs some celery for her chicken soup
and better get some challah

while she's at the store.

She can't remember knitting little dresses
in darkened movie theaters by the beach,
speedy fingers basting blue for my eyes
pearling pink for cousin Donna's olive skin.
My Grandma Lena crocheted shawls
and afgans, bedspreads, dainty doilies
and sweaters that still sparkle
in my dresser drawer
with aurora borealis beads.

Memories are stocked like her pantry
a supermarket supply of delight,
she no longer walks around
in her birthday suit
it's got more wrinkles than an old coat.

I laugh with my kids
about the day she went for her driver's license
and drove the car into the butcher shop,
paid the guy ten dollars
and walked away with the card and a grin.

Grandma no longer
squeezes Florida oranges at breakfast
but I can still feel
the thrill of her embrace.
She can finish off a carton of chow mein
demolish an entire lobster
and lick a Thanksgiving wishbone clean.

She doesn't have a coffee table
so she can't put out Brach candies
in her mother's cut glass dish.
Her hall smells like cafeteria
mixed with urine
instead of roasted chicken
rugelach, kugel and home.

It was at her apartment in Rockaway
on a rainy second grade afternoon
that I learned to snap my fingers

and work on my very own sweater vest.
As soon as grandpa came in for the night
from his jewelry shop
she'd get him his slippers
fetch the paper
pour soup in his favorite dish.
She only wanted to do what
Louie wanted next.

She doesn't believe
she rode a bus all the way to California
or opened her own bar and grill,
cooked peppers and onions for workmen
and fat steak fries sprinkled with paprika.

Years of cleaning statuettes
on gold leaf mirrored trays,
and portraits of those who died long ago
are clearer than the moosh
they gave her for lunch today.

Grandma Lena taught us all
about loving, family first
and finding humor in the midst of a storm.
We can still make her giggle
when we tell her the story about daddy
the time he rode a horse
up the steep steps to their house
and knocked on her front door.

She lights up when we enter the sunroom
recognizes us though she's
forgotten details like birthdays, names
and exactly who's married to who.
My aunt brings her bagels and herring
to remind her of all of the good times
glazed with lots of kisses and care.

On the phone, the day before Yom Kippur
I asked, "So what's your recipe for life?"
As always she simply answered
"With family there's always
something to laugh about,

I had an honest husband
and kids that were never ashamed of me.
Years spiced with closeness and plenty of love
especially Lindy, for you."

LYNDA CALABRESE is an artist/designer turned poet. A native of New York, she now lives in Charlotte, North Carolina, with her artist husband and two children. She teaches art and poetry at a transitional school for homeless children.

ELEGY FOR NANNIE

For Ruth Rosenberg Pereles

Janet Ruth Heller

I loved to visit you when I was a child.
Your closet was full of coloring books,
And you kept chewing gum for grandchildren
In your living room, next to decks of cards.
Your china lady would welcome us
By nodding her head and her hands.
You puffed smoke rings to amuse us,
But you whistled sad old tunes.

When I cooked with you, you never got angry,
Even if I couldn't separate eggs.
I can still taste your frosted cakes,
Your matza and eggs, your chicken with cherries,
And your black raspberry jam.

You took Will and me to Chicago
On the big yellow and green train
To shop for presents in December
And to see the animated exhibits at Field's.
Back home, you drove us all around Milwaukee
To see the homes with the best displays.

I like to remember you smiling
And laughing at my jokes
And generating quips of your own.
You said that an unfriendly doctor
Had "the personality of a goldfish."
You told a banking clerk
That, because of your arthritis,
You could never rob the vault,
Take the money, and run!
You claimed that if the University of Chicago
Withheld my Ph.D.,
You would move your aching body
To Illinois and "burn the school down."

"It's hard to go on living,"

You have told me for the last five years.
I'm glad you did go on
Despite losing one breast,
Despite the fiery cancer devouring your bones.

You lived to see me finish my Ph.D.,
And you walked down the aisle
At my wedding. You lived to cuddle
Nine great-grandchildren
And to hear the news that your tenth
Would be named after your Joe.

Though your body is in the ground,
Sometimes I feel your spirit near me,
Lighter, happier, even wiser,
Smiling and laughing
As I love to remember you.

JANET RUTH HELLER teaches English literature at Grand Valley State University in
Allendale, Michigan. Her poetry has appeared in many journals and anthologies. She is
a founding mother of *Primavera*, a women's literary magazine. Her book, *Coleridge,
Lamb, Hazlitt, and the Reader of Drama,* was published in 1990.

A VANISHING BREED
Joan Kramer

One of the least noted fallouts of the women's movement is the vanishing of grandmothers as we knew them. I am speaking of that lovable little old lady with the bun and bunions and the tray of warm cookies emerging from the oven.

Let me explain. My grandmother wore a mid-calf floral print dress (way before it was dubbed the midi) and sensible shoes and sat on the front porch of a southern frame house rocking and knitting and gossiping about the neighbors (as in: "Sadie always did have champagne taste and a beer pocketbook.") My grandmother had a green thumb and was proud of her pink azaleas and the fat scarlet tomatoes on her table, plucked fresh from her garden that morning. She grated her own horseradish.

My other grandmother was a regal, Ingrid Bergman type. After seeing *Anastasia,* my childhood imagination always fantasized her as the escaped daughter of the Russian imperial family. She spoke in broken English—I don't think she ever wrote the language—but was a shrewd, self-made business-woman and the creator of wonderful smells, of stuffed cabbage and noodle pudding, wafting from the kitchen. Living close by, she was a safe harbor when I ran away from home, for in her house I could do no wrong.

My son's grandmother wears what used to be called a skort and can usually be found on the eighteenth hole of a manicured green fairway playing "golf with the girls." That is when she's not dashing off to macrame at the community college or interior design at the shopping center or brunch at the latest hot spot. This grandmother, by the way, is the same mother who ferried her three children to and from school every time it rained and trembled at the thought that one of them might not marry a local boy and spawn precious little grandchildren for her to dote over. When they did, she picked up and moved to Florida for the winter.

My son's other grandmother announced—after years of scout leading, room mothering and staying home until all three of her children were *through* college (just in case one of them might want to drop in for the weekend)—that she had always nurtured a burning desire to be a real estate agent. Weekends are her busiest time. We practically had to call her office in the guise of prospective clients to negotiate her birthday dinner. The closest thing to a warm cookie my son has seen in her house is the inside of a Pepperidge Farm box hastily pulled from the deep freeze.

Now I have always prided myself on being thoroughly modern and must admit that my first reaction to these liberated, laissez-faire grandmothers was, "That's great." But is it?

I mean after all the glib jokes (My grandmother left Oriental rugs and antique glass; I guess my kids will be fighting over the lucite) and wry observations (Just think, a whole generation of grandchildren growing up without ever having sniffed homemade gingerbread) have been made, who benefits? Certainly not I, my son or his grandmothers. Maybe any grandmother (or mother, for that matter) who still has time to bake. A fortune lies waiting for the first person to patent scratch-and-sniff cards in three aromas (say, gingerbread, chocolate chip and deep-dish apple pie) for newfangled grannies to wave around their kitchens.

It may turn out when I am a grandmother that I will feel too old and tired to keep up with my grandchildren or too busy and flush with my newfound freedom to bother with them (Gee, wouldn't it be nice to learn Spanish, take a photography course, visit some of those exotic faraway places you've always dreamed about?) It may be that when they are babies, I will want to dress-'em-up-cute and show them off to my friends. And when their mother needs a break, I may cavalierly toss off, "I raised mine. Now it's your turn" or one of the other excuses I've heard. It may be that grandmothers will go the way of vestigial organs, which atrophy from lack of use.

But I hope not. For my grandmothers, despite their homespun homilies, inadvertently taught me what's missing from my own son's childhood. At their knee, I absorbed the mantle of tradition, a bit of wisdom, and something like unconditional love. I keep reminding my husband to remind me, when my son has children, that I want to be for them the kind of grandmother my grandmothers were for me.

JOAN KRAMER has been a full-time and freelance journalist in the Washington, D.C. area for seventeen years. Her travel articles have appeared in Sunday travel sections across the country. Her poetry has been published in many literary magazines. She also does community service work, such as leading a writing workshop at a runaway shelter and teaching English to refugees. She is married, has one son and lives in McLean, Virginia.

MY HEART KNOWS

To Grandma Jeanne on her 90th Birthday

Amy J. Gup

Grandma—what do you mean to me?
   You are what connects me to my culture.
      —to who I am, where I come from
      —to what it means to be Jewish
I have not received the Jewish education or upbringing
   that you wished I had
don't know a bit of Hebrew
But I catch myself now
using your Yiddish phrases, style of speech
From you
I carry the feeling inside that tells me
   beyond words or knowledge—that I am Jewish
My heart knows

Grandma—what do you mean to me?
You have given me the chutzpah it takes
   to get through life
You are not the quiet, demure, sweet grandmother
That is not your style
You flaunt your style
Wear it like a brightly-colored scarf for all to see
You are who you are and that's all there is to it
And who you are is strong, stubborn, ornery, funny
Tough-minded, thick-skinned, a "character"
As when you tap your canasta cards on the table impatiently
and say,"Let's go, all right already"
And that is how you have lived your life these 90 years

In those ways you have taught me strength
   —to roll with the punches
   —to be myself
   —to live my life as my own
I look in your eyes and see the years
   wonder what those eyes have seen
Once in a while you offer me a glimpse,
   a story of time past

But now you are living each day for itself
and there is no real way to tell a lifetime of experience

Grandma—what do you mean to me?
Love
The love of collecting my poems over the years
    in a special book
        —from eight-year-old scrawlings
        —to those I write today.
The love I hear in your voice
    when we talk on the phone
The love I feel
    when you rest your hand on my arm
The love in your eyes
    when the family would arrive at your door
    after midnight
    and you would come down the elevator in your bathrobe
    to greet us
The love in the special food
    you would have stocked in your tiny apartment—just for us
The love in the warmth
    of your hug
For the love you have given me
For the love I feel for you
I give you this poem

AMY J. GUP is a writer and musician from Oakland, California, where she plays electric bass with a local band. Her grandmother has been the main source of cultural inspiration in her life.

MILDY'S ATTIC
Carole Bellacera

In the spring of 1967, the Lincoln Junior High She-Devils Softball Team won the state championship and earned the right to go to San Francisco for the play-offs. I was a scrawny tomboy with frizzy red hair, a too-big Irish nose and chameleon eyes framed with colorless lashes. Nothing to look at, by any means, but I was the best third baseman in all of Kentucky. At least, that's what everybody told me.

Trouble was, I wouldn't be going to California with the rest of the team. Daddy was real sad about it; he was as proud of me as could be, but we just didn't have $300 to spare. Not with the farm going bad like it was. Of course, all the town merchants were helping out to send the team off, but there was only so much they could do. At a town meeting, it was agreed that the parents would have to come up with $300, and for most people, that wasn't such a huge amount. But the drought of the previous summer and the low snowfall this winter had made it near impossible for the farmers in the area to break even. That, combined with the cost of a new furnace and Grandma Mildy's hospitalization when she broke her hip the day after Christmas, had put the figurative nail on the coffin for my trip to San Francisco.

I didn't blame anybody for it. And what good would it have done to walk around with a long face because of it? Daddy worked hard in the fields, and mama did, too. I knew they felt like they were letting me down, so I tried to make them feel better by pretending that I didn't want to go to that old hippie state anyways. Heck, they might haul me away and turn me into one of them flower children. That's what I said to them at dinner one night, said it with a little laugh. They laughed, too, and pretended that they believed I was telling the truth. Of course, I *did* want to go to California. More than anything in the world. But facts were facts, and there was just no way we could get our hands on that kind of money. To get off the subject, I asked Grandma Mildy if she'd care for a slice of blackberry pie. She just loved blackberry pie. When I placed it in front of her, she smiled up at me sweetly and said, "Thank you kindly, Liz Beth."

Grandma Mildy (short for Mildred) suffered from senility. I guess they call it something else today. Alzheimer's disease, I think. But some days Grandma Mildy was just as sharp as any of us. On that night, she was.

I loved my mama, but sometimes she made me so mad when she talked about her own mother as if she weren't there. That's what she did after I took my seat back at the table. She looked over at my daddy and said, "I found her trying to get up in the attic again, Jack. I just don't know what I'm going to do with her."

I looked over at Grandma Mildy to see if she was listening, but she was busy eating up her pie.

"Short of tying her to her rocking chair, I don't know what we can do about it," daddy said.

Mama shook her head. "Now, you know I can't do that to her. I just wish she'd behave herself. All we need is for her to break another bone."

"Why is she so fascinated with the attic, anyway?" Daddy asked, helping himself to some more cornbread. "Them rickety steps are dangerous, even for Liz there. Can't imagine why an eighty-year-old woman would want to get up there, anyway."

"All her old photo albums are up there," I said. "Lots of pictures of her and Grandpa Charley when they were young."

"Well, if that's all she's after, you can haul 'em down for her after supper, Liz," mama said. She looked at Grandma Mildy and spoke in a louder tone. "Did you hear that, mom? Liz Beth is going to bring down your picture albums after supper."

Grandma Mildy smiled broadly. Little blackberry seeds clung to her dentures like polka dots on a summer dress. "She's a good girl, Liz Beth," she said.

After the supper dishes were washed up, I climbed up the narrow attic steps and brought down a couple of old leather-bound photo albums. Grandma Mildy and I settled into the front porch swing and leafed through them until dark. She didn't talk much that night, just studied the photos with a secret little smile. Not for the first time, I wondered what was going on in that sharp brain of hers.

Everybody in our family loved Grandma Mildy to death, but even my nine-year-old brother, Johnny, treated her like she was a two-year-old. I think I was the only one who thought there was a lot more going on with her than she let on. Yes, there were times when she was definitely confused, but I suspected there were other times when she acted more confused than she really was. I don't know how I knew that. Maybe it was something that danced in her cornflower blue eyes. Something that said, "Hey, Mildred Ann is still here, and she ain't going anywhere for a long time." I still don't know why she'd pretend to be senile when she wasn't, but I guess she had her reasons.

The next day was hot and humid, too hot and humid for late May. But after a long cold winter, we kids were slaphappy about it and along about one in the afternoon, Johnny and I took off for the creek with our innertubes. Our cousins, Pauline and Jake, who lived on the next farm, were already there in the middle of the stream. For a couple of hours, we splashed around and had a good old time. It was quite a while before we noticed how dark it was getting. Finally, there was a low rumble of thunder and I knew I'd best be getting Johnny back to the house. As we came over the hill, mama met us. Her face was gray with worry.

"Bad weather's coming," she said. "I'm gonna help your daddy round up the cattle." She glanced up at the dark bank of clouds coming in from the southwest. "All's we need now is to have lightning strike a bunch of them under a tree. Johnny, you come on with me. Liz Beth, your grandma is taking a nap. You go stay with her, but if you see a funnel cloud, you all get yourselves to the storm cellar. I reckon we'll be along soon."

As Johnny and mama took off for the fields, I broke into a run toward the house. If there was one thing in the world I was scared of, it was tornado weather. And I wasn't about to sit in the house waiting around to see a funnel cloud. There was only one thing in my mind, and that was to get Grandma Mildy up and get her in that storm cellar.

But when I burst into her bedroom, she wasn't there! I raced through the house. "Grandma Mildy! Where are you?" There was a flash of lightning outside, followed by a deafening crash of thunder. A hard rain began to fall. It was suddenly so dark inside that I could barely see my hand in front of my face. My heart was pounding with fear. I didn't know what to do. I couldn't go to the storm cellar without grandma, but where was she? That's when I thought of the attic.

I stumbled up the steps, nearly tripping in my haste. As I reached the top, a flash of lightning lit up the tiny room, and I saw Grandma Mildy on her knees in front of an old trunk. She was riffling through it and muttering.

"Grandma, come on. There's a bad storm coming. We need to go to the cellar."

She didn't look up. "I know they're in here somewheres," she said, removing a pile of clothing and sticking her hands in again.

"Grandma!" I felt like I was going to cry. "Please come on. I'm scared."

Finally, the words sank in and she turned to me, a serene look on her face. "Why Liz Beth, it's just a little old thunderstorm. No use getting all agitated about it." She turned back to the trunk. "Ah, here it is! Come on over here, honey. I got something to show you."

Quickly, I crossed to the tiny window that looked out over the backyard and saw that the sky was lightening up some. The rain was still falling at a heavy pace, but it *did* look like the worst was over. I took a deep shaky breath and moved over to Grandma Mildy.

"What is it, grandma?"

She was tugging what looked like a heavy book out of the bottom of the trunk. I reached in a hand to help her with it. With an "oomph" she dropped it to the floor and smiled. "I knew it was here. Your grandpa was proud as pie of this."

She opened the heavy book and pointed to a tarnished coin. "Do you know what this is, Liz Beth?" Her blue eyes were glass clear.

"An old coin," I said.

Grandma Mildy smiled. "Not just *any* old coin. This here is a genuine Confederate coin given to your great-great-grandpa by none other than Jeb Stuart."

"That's nice," I said, one ear on alert for changes in the sound of the storm outside.

"Your Grandpa Charley's grandpa was the only blacksmith in town during the War between the States, and one day when the Rebels were camped in the vicinity, Jeb Stuart came in to have his horse reshod. This was the coin he used to pay for it."

"Oh!" I tried to inflect my voice with enthusiasm, but I couldn't really understand Grandma Mildy's sudden interest in history. "Grandma, let's go on downstairs now. I think the storm is starting to let up."

It was true. The rumble of thunder was farther away now and the rain was beginning to slacken. But Grandma Mildy chose not to pay attention to my words. Her gnarled fingers slipped into the pocket of the book and dug out the coin. The next thing I knew, she had pressed it into my hand.

"Before he passed on, Charley told me that these coins are worth a lot of money. This one, alone, could fetch maybe $500." There was a faraway look in her eyes, yet, somehow, she looked younger, and for the first time, I caught a fleeting glimpse of the young woman she'd been when she'd first married my grandpa. "I always wanted to go to San Francisco. Or anywheres, for that matter. But the closest I ever got to a fancy place like that was a weekend in Cincinnati." She closed my fingers around the coin and held my hand tight in hers. "I want you to have your daddy take this to one of them places in Lexington and exchange it for cash. Then you can have your trip to San Francisco."

"But grandma! This coin has been in your family for generations. I couldn't sell it just so I can see San Francisco."

Her face grew stern. "And may I ask what good it's doing gathering dust up here in this old attic? Don't you think we'd be selfish if we didn't share it with others? Now, listen here, Liz Beth. I don't want to hear no more about it. You're going to San Francisco and that's that. What's more, your grandpa would've wanted you to do it."

I doubted that most assuredly, but I didn't say so. My face must have revealed my uncertainty because Grandma Mildy suddenly decided to pour on the Irish charm.

"Do it for me, Liz Beth. I want to sit out on the swing and think of you seeing all them pretty places there. You can send me a postcard of the Golden Gate Bridge! Oh, I declare, that would just tickle me to death."

What could I say? My sweet grandma had risked her fragile bones to climb up here just to give me this old coin. A rush of tenderness ran through me, and I gave her a hug.

"Oh, grandma, I *do* love you!"

She smiled tremulously. "So, you'll use this to go?"

"If daddy says it's okay," I said. "Oh, yeah. There *is* a condition, though."

A little frown crossed her face. "Now, I don't care too much for conditions. I'm at an age where such things run counter to me."

I folded my arms across my chest and gave her a stern look "Then I *won't* go."

"Okay, missy, what's your condition?"

"That you don't climb up these stairs again. Ever." I leaned over to place a kiss on her papery cheek. She smelled vaguely of rose water and lavender. "If you need anything up here, just ask me. I'll get it for you. Okay?"

Grandma Mildy smiled and reached out to brush a lock of my copper hair away from my eyes. "We have a bargain, Liz Beth." And she stuck out her mottled hand for us to shake on it.

I helped her to her feet. "Come on, now. The storm is over. We'll go downstairs and bake some cookies or something."

With a secure hand on her arm, I helped Grandma Mildy down the narrow attic stairs.

She never looked back.

CAROLE BELLACERA's fiction has appeared in magazines such as *Off Duty America, The Family* and *Mississippi Review.* Her first children's picture book, *The Taming of the Troll,* is scheduled for publication by Bantam Doubleday Dell in October 1993. She recently moved from Honolulu to the Washington, D.C. area.

IN MEMORY OF CLAUDIA HARRIS, 1898-1981
Ingrid Reti

You were the grandmother I longed for
when I came looking for a room.
You showed me the upstairs front room
with the old maple peering in the window,
told me about your husband's recent death,
introduced me to your other roomer, Miss Boyden.

You were the grandmother I longed for.
I came to you, a bird with a damaged wing
disillusioned by life, by marriage;
you enfolded me in your warmth
but asked few questions
until like a flower
I unfolded of my own accord.

You were the grandmother I longed for.
Your home was quiet, calm, restful
a two-story white frame
set in the midst of similar suburban New England houses
surrounded by lawns that you feared
would never stop threatening to go to seed.

You were the grandmother I longed for.
You chided me gently
for not telling you about my birthday
sat and talked with me about books, ideas
read me your poetry
told me of your life long ago in Greenwich Village.
You missed Jim, your husband, talked of him often
and yet I could not picture you with him.

You were the grandmother I longed for.
Your face was lined with the beauty of age
but to me you were ageless.
You made my friends feel welcome
enjoyed their company as they did yours.

You were the grandmother I longed for.
You told me once that I was a cold fish;
your warmth melted my frozen spirit.
I loved, admired and respected you
and decided that if ever I had children
you would be my model.

You were the grandmother I longed for
and I think for you
I was the granddaughter you never had.
You called me "chickadee"
told me Andy was stubborn but liked his charm
came to my wedding in a bright red suit
were dubbed "Madame Senator" by Andy's mother
so impressed was she with your regal bearing.

The time came when I left you
grandmother I had longed for
my wings were mended.
You came to New York with me
to see me off for Venezuela.
Did I leave a void in your life?
I know that you missed me,
but strong woman that you were
you did not grieve
found new interests
in your relationship with Charley
who moved into my room.

Grandmother that I longed for
the years passed,
I shared my life with you in letters
called you often and told you about my children
and how much I loved you, but those last six years
could not bring myself to fly to see you
for then I would have had to tell you
that my life with Andy was over.
I wanted to spare you that pain.

Grandmother that I longed for
death carried you away
at the age of 103
but in my life you live on
Madame Senator, Claudia
Grandmother that I longed for.

INGRID RETI is a literature and creative writing instructor at California Polytechnic State University, Extended Education in San Luis Obispo, California. She produces and hosts a weekly TV show, *On Books and Authors*. Her poetry has appeared in numerous literary magazines. *Echoes of Silence,* her second collection of poetry, was published in 1990.

SLICE
Jenna Day

"I want to stay at grandma's," I pleaded as they left.
"Well, all right. If it's no trouble, mom," says daddy.
"Just remember, sometimes she still, ahem, you know, the bed."

Grandma laughs and smiles and reassures the big man
whose diapers she once washed by hand.

"She won't."

"Bye mommy, bye daddy."
Kiss. Kiss good-bye.
Goodbye brave new world of post-Apollo and dishwashers.

Welcome.
Welcome the woodfire. The days of grandma.

By grandpa's knee that night, licking blueberry pie
from a fork with grandma's initials on it, I say,
"Nana, were you ever little?"

Laugh.
Laugh.
The sound of old people, distant and wise,
Fills the room and curls up the chimney with the wood smoke.

"Why, yes, of course.
When we grew up, we had very little, and we had to work hard.
I had only one doll," says grandma, softly. "She had a rag
Face and yarn for hair...but to me...she was beautiful."

"Back in the old days, we knew what work was," says grandpa, as
he gets up to go to bed.

I curl in between them in the warm feather bed.

"She should sleep in the next room," says grampie.
"Oh, just tonight," replies his girl of fifty years.

She puts her arms around me.
Her nightie smells like Ben-Gay.
Her hair is soft and dry...like wool.
Her permanent from Grants tucked in a hairnet.

I lie, pressed between them in the too warm house, like a precious autumn leaf, encased between the pages of two old, seldom read books.

I sleep, like grandma's only doll, on a rolling sea of wild blueberries.
Tonight, as the soft smoke curls upward,
I do not pee.

JENNA DAY is a housewife and mother of two boys. She was born in East Fryeburg, Maine, where she is currently working on her B.A. in social sciences. Her writing has appeared in *Down East* magazine and in numerous college publications.

ADORATION
Ayesha Maqueda Vashti

I once fantasized she was really my mama—
    (Gave me to mother because she was old and husbandless).

I'd sit in my sanctuary—in granma's room,
    In her rocking chair,
    In her memories.

Granma—tall, honey brown, Indian cheekbones
    Indian black braids laced with silvery silk strands.

Granma—soft brown hands decorated with large age spots.
    Old hands—once hard working hands,
        Changing babies' diapers hands,
        Wiping snotty noses hands,
        Scrubbing clothes on scrub board hands.

She once was young you know.
    Younger than I am now.
Had boyfriends, boyfriends great-granma and great-granpa liked,
    But she didn't
One boyfriend she liked, but they didn't
So she married him—
    The one she did and they didn't
That was some day all those many years ago.
    A day that scandal danced about:

      "Did you hear bout Will and Alice Crawley's May Lizzie
        And Will and Betty Newman's John runnin off like that?
        Runnin off and gettin married like that?
        What the young folks won't do these days.
        Why in our time…"

They all knew:
    Knew Will Crawley thought his Lizzie was too good for young John;
    Knew Will Newman didn't want to see any of his ten kids get married,
        Cause they had to care for him in his old age.

It took a year and one fuzzy headed baby boy to join these two
        Families together.

I babysat with granma—or whatever one calls it when the child put into one's
charge is a seventy-nine-year-old, second childhood child.

I bathed granma, fascinated by her naked body,
        Fascinated by her flaccid pendular breasts
        Where once nestled husband and suckled child,
        Fascinated by the long black hairs curtaining off the
        Aged portals that once gave carte blanche to love and life.
I teased granma about opening her legs so eagerly to allow the water to play
        in her "stuff."
        I asked her if young John found her so eagerly accommodating.
She gave me an impish smile as she told me how:

        "He used to make me sick.
        Couldn't go anywhere with him overnight.
        He always wanted it—why I recall one time in particular
            At his sister's house.
        I was afraid everybody in the house would hear."

She married him to get away from home,
        To have someone to take care of her.
And he did take good care of her
            Until death, in the form of a coal mine
Took him away from her and their eight children.
She never married again, never had any boyfriends again.
A part of her died and was buried with young John.

I was granma's favorite—her Kathy.
That's what she called me then.
I called her Mang.
"Your hair is your crowning glory," she told me.
She told me that I was beautiful.
In church one Sunday some girls sitting behind mother and granma were talking
about me
        (They didn't know she was my granma)
"That girl sure thinks she's cute," said one.
"I know she does, but she ain't," said the other.
"Oh yes she is," said granma as she turned around to face them

106

"And you are," she said as mother recounted the story to me.

Granma adores me as I adore her.
I once fantasized she was really my mama.
I'm babysitting granma.
I'm changing granma's diaper now.

AYESHA MAQUEDA VASHTI of Paterson, New Jersey, summarizes her life's goal in the following way: "Once on hearing of a society in which it is the privileged obligation of the elders to sit beneath an aged spreading oak disbursing their knowledge and lore among the youth, I began to yearn to sit one day beneath that oak, with wisdom enough to partake as well as disburse."

107

FOR THE LADY WHO NEVER SCREAMED AT ME AND SMELLED OF SUGAR
Dorothy Peterson Cooke

I watched you, old woman, at your dying,
Your frail frame hardly made a lump
On the altar of the sterile bed.
Your mouth made sucking sounds,
And wrinkled flesh
Hung from your bone arms.
The world was whispers
And moved on soundless shoes
At your dying.

You were always in your sugar kitchen, nana.
Your hands would reach down to touch my hair.
You loved the smell of sunshine in my hair, you said.
We would have tea,
In the cups that scraped like seashells,
And just a taste of the dinner rice pudding.

Looking at the altar and the starch white you,
I could not speak.
But did you hear my love sounds
In the sugar smelling, seashell kitchen, nana?

DOROTHY PETERSON COOKE is a teacher who grew up on an island off the coast of Maine. Her work has appeared in *Down East Magazine* and *The Bar Harbor Times*. A grandmother herself now, DOROTHY COOKE shares with her students stories of people and events from her childhood.

REMEMBERING MAMIE
Patricia Smith Ranzoni

The tendency is to echo,
"They don't come like that anymore,"
which is what the doctors, nurses and anyone
who came to know her remarkable strength said.
Hattie Snowman Dunbar. Mamie.
Daughter of a captain of the sea
with a Maine mother to match.
She navigated her long life with courage,
pride and a fierce independence—
some called stubbornness—we recognize
as our Yankee heritage.
Oh, she was a *grand* grandmother!

Tall in stature, she lifted us to the height
of her spirit in work and play.
She took us by the hand and taught us.
She sang us lullabies
that can't be found in books.
She took us into her bed for riddle times
and into her heart in a way we never doubted.
Oh, she was a *grand* grandmother!

She was walks to the spring
and red net popcorn bags on the Christmas tree.
She was pulling out chairs for one another at table
and hot oatmeal with cream.
She was treats in the silver drawer
and card parties with lady friends
and prizes for good children.
She was a time of featherbeds,
kerosene lamps, and a pendulum clock
marking time (when there was enough time)
on the mantel.

Her time is not over.
Part of us has gone with her. Part
lives in us even as we say good-bye
to her tired body.

She took care of hers and others'
for as long as she could, and longer,
like the mittens she knit for us
as long as she could see, and longer.
If work be the measure of a person,
I see her in her apron this day, rewarded
with rest from the worry of that work
that she did as long as she could, and longer.

She grew to be what they call today
in magazine articles, "a salty old woman,"
survivor of nearly a century of change.
She didn't ask for much:
to see those she loved,
something chocolate once in a while,
and that her dresses come a respectable
length below her knees. But what she gave
we will have always:
a dignity in life and death, an example
of how to grow old with your head high,
knowing you have done your best
for as long as you could, and longer.
Oh, she was a *grand* grandmother!

"Work hard and long," she said,
"and someday your door will open."
At the end, which we believe was a
beginning because Mamie saw
what we've heard called the Promised Light,
she reached out and said,
"You know me.
Won't you open the door
and let me see how pretty it is?"
Oh, she was a *grand* grandmother!

Her grandmother's table was PATRICIA SMITH RANZONI's first home desk when, adapting to disability, she turned from a career in education and mental health to freelance writing. Now living in Bucksport, Maine, she sings "lullabies that can't be found in books" to her grandchildren. Her poetry appears frequently in Maine and national publications.

I SEND YOU WORD
for Ashley
Darcy Gottlieb

Grandmother,
I send you word of one
who has come to carry on
our matriarchal line
begun with your history
of an orphan's early marriage,
travel across mountains
through Indian territory
from Boston to vast acreage
set down in western land.

Where you rode bareback,
learned to oversee fruit orchards
wield an ax to cut firewood
and chop off the heads
of chickens. Where you knew
how to distract rattlesnakes
and once confronted a lion
on the muddy streets of Oregon.

Later, left to manage
the farm alone, a widow
with two young children
you fought off the hired man
when he tried to rape you
turned down marriage offers
so you might hold your reign.

Now she comes
this new girl-child
of the fifth generation
to join our tribe—
a budlet cast in female armor
who will be sovereign
in her own time
her eyes already intent
on subduing the world
as she learns its ways.

DARCY GOTTLIEB of Coral Gables, Florida, teaches at the University of Miami. She is also working on a libretto for an opera based on the Tiananmen Square massacre. DARCY GOTTLIEB is the winner of the Dylan Thomas and Christopher Morley Awards given by The Poetry Society of America. Widely published, she has given readings at the Folger Library and has conducted a number of workshops.

MY GRANDMOTHER'S HANDS
Carol Barrett

are happy stained with huckleberries,
pebbled fruit finespun as the Colorado
columbine she and grandpa picked
that first long summer. Now she has a son
who will take her to the mountains,
Crisco buckets bumping her lap
on the windy climb. She has friends
who have no son. She will bring them
a bluejay's feather, a bucket of berries.

Short and deliberate, my grandmother's hands
drench stalks of fresh dill alongside
fat cucumbers. Knuckles, wide as bunions
from her brother's shoes that never fit,
hold her rings in place in hot suds.
Her nails are lined like the ribs
of corduroy scraps she cuts into circle
skirts for my dolls, her fingers
knotting the very tips of the thread.
We snap and unsnap these soft wraps.

Raised on nickel loaves of bread,
she needs but one pair of shears, or hose,
one gray winter coat. She snips the brown-
fringed dahlias from their toothless stems,
cuts chives, beans, lettuce, string,
all with the scissors that clipped
her babies' hair, kitchen bowl at the bangs.
For breakfast, her hands squeeze cold oranges
into cheese jars—blue and white tulips,
or a woman in a red dress, cranking the phone.
The insides of the peels are slick. You drink
this juice with a spoon, you chew it down.

On Sundays my grandmother's hands
clutch a smart black bag. Change purse
popping like her snapdragons, maroon
and yellow jaws, she extracts her due,

matching the tone of the preacher's voice.
She's known for a good ear. At the piano
she trusts what is true, her hands
sorting the stacks: *You Never Walk Alone,*
Danny Boy, Bless This House. Above polished
keys, Hummels, gone fishing, whistle
for the dog, do their sums on a chalk
slate, pucker up on a park bench.
Sundays are certain, kiss or no.

Monday morning these hands will slide
halved apricots down Mason jars, scalloped
like vanilla wafers on a gingerbread roof.
They'll push the lawnmower which cackles
like a flock of camp robbers, heap mounds
of rummy clippings in a grocery bag,
sprinkle them, green ashes, over the rosebed.
She never stops feeding the hungry.
An hour before dusk her hands go out
to thin the carrots. She doesn't like
a crowd, savors the warm soil on her thumbs,
never breaks their parsleyed heads.
The tiniest, rinsed with a hose,
fill the house as it grows dark,
a hint of honeysuckle, yellow plum.

After the evening's last glass of milk,
my grandmother's needles knit in Morse code.
Skeins of yarn talk to me, sleep
winding up the stairs: Priscilla
is busy today-ay-ay, Daddy's gone a hunting,
bye bye bunting. Once the main road
washed out in the flood in Kalama,
picnic tables floating legs up. She lay
a thick quilt under my chin. All night:
the warm attic smell of safety.

I have only once watched my grandmother's hands
grieving. They wrung a rosy handkerchief
til the petals fell. She got down
on her knees and swept up the dry
hydrangea blooms, thin as moth wings,

floated them on the compost pile
over the egg shells and orange peels, then
waited for the mulch to ripen, the feet
of rosebushes soaking in the spring rain.

After long walks, my grandmother's hands
press wild grasses, clover, forget-me-nots,
encyclopedias filled with solitary sprigs
of wisdom pungent on the page. While I piece
a puzzle map of the world, she mixes
cinnamon biscuits, then returns to work
the blue edge of the sea, her fingers
bearing the light dust of flour
from the bottom of the pan.
At Chinese checkers, her hands fold in
to each other, studying the set.
She never moves back once the play
is out, even, when older, I show her
a jump she has missed. She will take
her hands' choices, win or lose.
She knows her man, always picks blue.

Tonight she will stoke the fire, stoop
to the sputtering sparks, turn
the calendar, so they can get the date
right, if they must. These hands
have no fear of what needs doing,
only of what needs nothing at all.

CAROL BARRETT of San Antonio, Texas, won an N.E.A. fellowship in poetry for 1991. Her poems appear in eighty literary magazines and a variety of anthologies and multidisciplinary publications. Growing up, she spent part of every summer with her grandmother, Caroline Clark, of Battleground, Washington, now 93.

WAITING FOR YOUR BIRTHDAY
for Grandma Ruebe

Barbara J. Mayer

I took my first coffee break
at your red formica kitchen table,
over a plate of Lorna Doones
and date nut bread. You warned
that caffeine would stunt my growth,
but I swallowed it anyway, creamy
with half-and-half, soggy with
dunked cookies. Sure enough,
I grew up petite like you, but without
the fierceness that moved you to heft
your pocketbook at a mugger. Even fleas
hopped for cover when your deft fingers
parted the fur on our collie's belly.
I remember the Saturday night
you bathed me and listened to my dismay
at hair sprouting in secret places.
"Be satisfied with yourself," was all
you said, wrapping me like a gift
in white terrycloth.
All those New Year's Eves
we popped corn on top of the stove,
watched Guy Lombardo and waited
for the champagne and ticker-tape,
the world uncorking your birthday.

BARBARA J. MAYER is a Chicago native and former journalist whose poetry and fiction have appeared in *Thema, The Lyricist, Keystone, Sanskrit, Thursday' s Child* and *Columbus Single Scene*. A resident of Mooresville, North Carolina, she works as a staff writer at nearby Davidson College.

LEGACY OF LOVE
Louise Hess

It seemed ironic that I'd be telling her how to take care of that plant when she had always had the front window of her railroad apartment filled with thriving plants, as frustrated gardeners do when they live in the city. Nevertheless, we made small talk about the begonia I had brought to the nursing home until suddenly she became silent, then asked, "Missus, do you have children?"

"Yes, grandma, I have two children, Carol and Billy, your great-grandchildren."

"Oh, how nice," she replied, then added wistfully, "I wish I had children." Her voice was low, her gaze was beyond me—perhaps already on eternity. That was the last time I saw her alive, but my memories of her are very distinct and they often sustain me.

She was born in 1895, in a small village outside of Lvov, in the Ukraine. Because the family was poor, her brother Edward left home to find a job in America. He settled in Pennsylvania and each time he sent money home to help support the family, a little was set aside for Mary, my grandmother. When she had saved enough money, preparations were made for her to join Edward. She was fourteen years old when she kissed her family good-bye and sailed off to the United States, never to see any of them again.

Exhausted after weeks at sea and clearance through Ellis Island, she anxiously searched the crowded New York dock for her brother. The name tag pinned to her thin coat helped Edward find her, but after their tearful reunion he told her he could not afford to take her back to Pennsylvania and had arranged for her to stay with a family in New York. She would have to share a room with three children in the family and help take care of them, in addition to the job they had found for her as a dishwasher. The restaurant job paid very little, but allowed her to have one full meal a day. With these basic needs taken care of, Edward left.

I can imagine how Mary must have felt being all alone in a new country, not knowing the language, homesick for her family, and afraid of what life with strangers would be like. As she climbed the steep tenement steps that night, her resolution to survive grew. She would be fine she decided; after all, she was in America. There was no gold in the streets as she had heard, but she had a job, and tomorrow she would become a fourteen-year-old independent working woman.

Mary worked hard and gradually adjusted to the ways of her new country. Somewhere along the way she met and married Theodore, my grandfather. One of my cousins believes it was an arranged marriage and that may have been so.

I recall seeing a large sepia wedding photograph hanging in a spare bedroom. The bride, only sixteen, wore a simple white voile wedding dress with a handkerchief hem and held a single white blossom attached to a beribboned prayer book. She stood in the classic pose of that era, resting one hand on the shoulder of the handsome, blond groom seated next to her. I hope it was a marriage of love; I know she had a hard life, so I like to think she was happy in her marriage.

She had four children: the first, Joanna, died of blood poisoning when she was two years old; the second, Anna, became my mother; the third, Katerina, became my Aunt Kitty; and the fourth, Nicholas, died in a subway accident when he was seventeen years old. The years after Nicky's death were terrible. Theodore drank heavily, lost his business, and eventually took his own life. Mary, who had always worked at a variety of menial jobs to help support the family, continued to work to pay off their debts and to support herself. She never learned to read or write in English, but learned enough to get her citizenship papers, then never failed to vote. Although she spoke English to her grandchildren and to those outside of the home, she would lapse into Ukrainian whenever she didn't want someone to know what she was talking about, and I quickly learned to understand Ukrainian so I wouldn't miss any of those tidbits.

She had three grandchildren—all granddaughters. We three cousins loved to visit grandma, who always had special treats for us, or wonderful ethnic foods, or her cure-all—tea with honey, laced with her blueberry wine. Even now I find that drink comforting when I'm not feeling well. Many of my sayings were born in her kitchen, and I often find myself repeating her favorite one: "If you don't use your head, you'll have to use your hands." She used to cook the same meal every Saturday: steak seared in a hot, dry iron skillet sprinkled with coarse salt, mashed potatoes with fried onions, sour pickles and buttered rye bread. That is still one of my favorite meals.

Whenever I stayed overnight, I'd sleep with her in a soft feather bed with huge feather pillows and she'd smell of the cold cream she unfailingly rubbed on her face each night. In the morning, she would scramble eggs in a small iron pan and let me eat out of the pan. She used to let me play with her coral necklace (I always thought it looked like a string of chow mein noodles) and let me try on her only other piece of jewelry—an oversized gold bangle bracelet called a "slave bracelet" which was worn on the upper arm in the flapper style popular in the 1920's. It was simply inscribed with "Theodore." One time while she was babysitting, I strayed away from her as I followed a kitten into the street and didn't hear her warning as a coal truck barreled down the street towards me. With only seconds to react, she pushed me face down—out of harm's way— saving my life. We clung together relieved but shaken. After hugging and kissing me she wiped away the blood mixed with both our tears then gave me a good smack on the bottom. The next morning, as I sat with swollen lips and raccoon-like eyes, I got a long lecture about running into the street.

I can still see her in my mind's eye, not as she was that last time in the nursing home, but as she watched me in the mirror while I'd comb out her hair, or as she stood by the kitchen coal stove spoon-feeding a sick animal, or as she sat by that plant-filled window, watching the world go by. I've passed her apartment building several times in the last twenty years and I always look up at her window. I know she's not there but I feel compelled to check anyway.

These, and other treasured memories, are the only mementos I have of her. Her legacy to me was what I needed most—her love. I admired her strength of character and her capacity to make me feel loved no matter how brusque her manner, and I hope I am as strong and loving as she was. How often I wish she were here to hug me, how often I long for those rough red hands to brush away my tears, how often I thank God she was a part of my life.

A native of New York City, LOUISE HESS lives in Cincinnati, Ohio. She is a wife, mother, grandmother, homemaker and part-time college student majoring in women's studies. LOUISE HESS has been writing prose and poetry since returning to college four years ago. Her poetry has been published in several issues of *Perspectives,* a yearly literary journal by non-traditional students. This is her first non-fiction piece.

EVEN THE BIRDS
Sarah Singer

This poem is for you,
Grandma, whose voice
Caressed my name,
Who tendered love
And the benediction
Of bread and butter
As soon as I came.

We'd speak of your shtetl,
And how you baked bread
When your children were small,
And hid the extra loaves.
"There was never enough," you said.
"Before the week was out,
They'd found them all."

Assured me: "Child,
That was long ago.
There's enough now."
Would pour milk
Into a tall glass,
And fuss and flutter
Around me yet again.

Today, replete,
My children hoard buns
And leftover bread
To toss out on the snow.
Ours such surfeit,
I wish you could know
Even the birds are fed.

SARAH SINGER of Seattle, Washington, has recently been awarded prizes by The Washington Poets Association, the Seattle branch of The National League of American Penwomen, and the Portland branch of The Penwomen. Her third book, entitled *The Gathering,* was published in 1991.

TEA IN THE PARLOR OR FISH FOR BREAKFAST
Annette Johns

Grandma Leonard was intelligent and refined—
as elegant in her clean pressed apron
as in the lavender lace dress
she wore at my wedding
and her funeral.
Distant and mysterious,
she always sat or stood
as if she were posing for a portrait
by John Singer Sargent.
She looked taller than she was, crowned
with silver braids on a head held high.
I imagined her to be an opera singer
in concert, standing beside a grand piano—
my own very grand grandmother.
One summer I stayed with her,
and one night was late getting in.
I did not expect to find her up
but there she was, waiting—
like a statue, she sat and said nothing.
I mumbled the usual excuses.
She rose, finally, said nothing
and went to bed.
I saw, empty there, her perfect partner—
the enormous leather and wood carved
lion-footed chair.
In the morning and again
after my life-guard lesson at the lake,
I would take the chair across from her
and we would have tea together
in the front parlor.
I loved to listen to her past—
left motherless at seven,
she took care of the younger children
while her librarian father
read late into the night.
After high school she eloped
with a nobody, my grandfather,

who died when I was three.
A trace of Scotland was at home
on her tongue and precise diction
gave her prominent chin
a fine sense of belonging.
Her face was lined and underlined
like a lovely rare old book.
And I, her favorite,
longed to be like her.

Grandma Schram was never aproned,
but baked pies and bread
that always made my eyes
bigger than my stomach.
The smell of molasses and yeast
never left her, whether she was out fishing
on Galloway Lake early in the morning,
or singing on Sunday in the Baptist church.
She laughed and cried easily—in the open,
even with me, and never seemed ashamed.
I heard her pray and saw her read
her King James Bible often.
She quoted her favorite verses so naturally
that it did not occur to me the words
were not all her own.
She would say of my father,
"This is my beloved son
with whom I am well-pleased."
And she was pleased with everyone,
especially me. She gave Uncle Johnny,
the bum, a bed. But she saved me
from my parents—explaining
how I could do no wrong.
Sometimes I was caught off guard
by how hard she hugged or patted me.
Maybe she wanted to convince me
that I could be less aloof, more free.
I'm glad now that she never noticed
how often I was embarrassed
by her gum chewing, yawns, or loud "amen!"
She was oblivious to my blush or my silence.

And, if anything, hugged me a little harder.
I began to see that no one could come
between her and her energy.
After picking huckleberries all day
we'd go home and start the pies.
She'd roll out the dough,
mixing her instructions with jokes
I only partly understood.
Then, teasing and coaxing me
to take and eat more candy,
she filled my pockets and my childhood
with fantastic fun.
She had a creative vision
through those thick steamy glasses—
to make me, her favorite,
look easy to love.

ANNETTE JOHNS of Sycamore, Illinois, performs as an actress in community, university and professional theaters. An instructor of philosophy, she has recently co-translated a book of religious poems from Slovak.

CONTRADICTIONS
Anne Scott

I saw the two old women staring in the window of the antique shop. They were short and had on cotton print dresses under their heavy coats. Their shoes were sensible and their heads covered with knit caps. They were not unusual and I don't know why I stopped. They spoke to each other rather excitedly about the contents of the display. One seemed to recall a set of delicately flowered china that looked like a pattern from her mother's house. The other reminisced about a cranberry-colored glass bowl. They shared their memories of the various pieces and I stood in the doorway and listened. They didn't really remind me of my grandmother except in age and that wasn't quite true either. She would have been a little older than they. She died at seventy-two and that had been fourteen years ago.

I watched, wondering why I was eavesdropping on these two unsuspecting ladies and making comparisons. My grandmother was tall, not short. She never wore cotton print dresses except at home. She even called them "housedresses." She wore hats with flowers over her lavender blue hair and her shoes complemented her long legs.

She may have had some of the same glassware in her house and a teacup or two, but her china was different and it was pink. How odd I would remember her china so clearly. The shape of the dishes and cups; the design of each. How funny the color, how unlike the other memories of her.

Her summer garden was filled with flowers and butterflies of varying hues floating from one fragrant color to another. Playing there had been like visiting other worlds. One section, with only flowers and lawn, another with brick walks and green bushes; another with clotheslines and trellises of baby roses. An arbor of white filled with trailing green and yellow ivy led to her vegetable and fruit garden; there the brown dirt clutched at your bare toes as you reached for a small warm tomato or a hidden raspberry.

The patio with its three covered swings was her special place on those summer evenings, rocking and crocheting or rocking and praying, waiting for her daughters to arrive.

She wore her "housedresses" then. Dresses for home. Her cotton prints for wearing while washing her clothes with the wringer machine; lifting the heavy water-filled clothes, turning the roller, pulling the flattened clothes through. I helped her pull for I was too small for the lifting and turning.

Her house was different from the garden. The outside, she left for herself and her clean white wash. Inside, with few exceptions, was my grandfather's. A large television set, big chairs and the smell of hearty food baking; not the light scent of flowers. There were no vases of flowers, her touches here were the statues and crucifixes. Her concession to the outdoors was the dried palm leaves, blessed by the church and stuck behind her religious pictures. On her bedside table was a turquoise blue bottle with a silver cap, filled with holy water. I spent my early summers with her and some of the earliest days of my life and watched as she blessed herself with the holy water each night before we knelt by her bed for the last prayer of the day. That though, is another story. This is one of my grandmother, her lavender blue hair, her garden and her religion.

It is not of two old women and delicately flowered china, except, perhaps for a moment when their print dresses caught the reflection of a plate glass window and I thought I was a child again. I heard my young voice as I tugged at her dress, "Grandma, are my brothers coming today? Is mother coming today?"

❖❖❖

The office was filled with a yellow glare from the fluorescent lighting in the ceiling. The kind that crowds under simulated glass and is made up of long tubes suspended from a real ceiling. I checked my make up. The light made my face seem green and my lipstick pale. I thought about redoing something; but I knew the light in the inner office was not harsh.

The door opened and he motioned me inside. Dr. Chan was young, about thirty-five. He and I had been meeting for two years now and I liked him. He made me feel I was getting my money's worth. And sympathy was what it was all about.

The only thing I didn't like about him was that he made me do all the talking. I even had to choose the subject matter. Since I would spend my fifty minute hour chatting about a party I had attended where I wasn't sure if everyone really thought I was wonderful, or how my husband only liked Beethoven and I adored Mozart, the process was slow. But, he was always interested in my relationships with my family and he always perked up when I mentioned that I had seen a relative. He was interested in that.

I think he was a Freudian because he once launched into a long speech about Freud and a series of little stumbling blocks which always seemed to stand in the way of the next phase of one's psychic development; or at least that's what I think he said. He made me nervous when he got off the track and talked about personal issues. I just wanted to chat and not think of anything real or disturbing.

"My God, but that's what we're here for, because those are the issues that need discussing, not your social life," he said. "Tell me about your mother, your father. Anything. How you felt, what was special. Let's work at this."

"Jesus Christ," I answered, "what do you mean, what was special? Nothing, absolutely nothing. They didn't like me. Can't you tell? Jesus, Chan," (Jesus was a favorite word of mine). "That's why I'm here, they didn't like me and they ruined my life. How the hell am I supposed to tell you how I felt? It isn't important now. It was too long ago. Nothing Chan, old boy, I felt nothing, nothing, nothing. Oh hell, I hate the pictures you have on the wall. When are you going to do something about them?" I asked.

I didn't bother to tell him I was really asking that other question, "Grandma are my brothers coming today? Is my mother coming today?"

"Yes, she is, she comes every day. You know that," she replied.

Yes, I knew that. She came every day to visit grandma. I was pretty sure she wasn't coming to see me because she also spent the five days each week, during the school year, visiting grandma, but not the weekends. Yeah, I knew she was coming. Big deal. Pretty soon the summer would be over and I would be back at her house. Then she wouldn't have to pretend.

I felt unsafe when she was there. Things changed. She watched me. She criticized me. "What are you doing? Are you playing with your dolls? What game? Why are you sitting in the dirt?

"Come to the store with me. Your grandmother will watch your brothers. Well, maybe she'll ride with us; but they can wait in the car. I only need a few things today. Maybe I'll buy you ice cream for later," she said.

Why was she always trying to take me away? I wasn't sad when she left, but not glad either. It was okay.

"Grandma, why doesn't she like my prayers?" I asked. "The car didn't start and I said a 'Hail Mary'. You said it was always a good thing to do, to pray to the Blessed Virgin. But she laughed, not even nicely and said, 'Don't be silly. Don't do that.' I thought I was supposed to pray when things went wrong. Isn't that right, grandma, that's what you would have done wasn't it?" I asked.

"So you see, Chan, there's no point in any of this. My mother didn't even like the prayers of a child. She laughed."

❖❖❖

They were ugly pictures. One multi-colored abstract that was made up of a series of tiny dots. It made you dizzy if you looked at it long enough. Like looking at the past.

A grandmother with lavender blue hair who was always nice to me, who prayed to her angels and made my favorite pies each Sunday. Summers of wonderfully long days and fairy tale games of princesses and dolls.

A series of small dots, sometimes forming a picture and sometimes only a blob of color. Like the marble vein in the communion rail at church. I sat in the front row with grandma at my grandfather's funeral remembering the games I used to play to pass the time. Searching the pattern of the white and gray marble, looking for the familiar patterns I envisioned while staring ahead, never turning. They were still there, the face of an old man, the shadow of a horse, the snow-capped top of a mountain range. They were still there etched in that huge block of stone and my grandfather was being buried and how she wished she had gone with him.

I wondered what she would do now, alone. She sat in her living room that morning and cried. She told me how she loved to dance and how he hated dancing. They would have been married fifty years that October and she had wanted him to dance with her on their anniversary.

After the funeral, she never slept in the house again. She stayed with one of her daughters each night for the next several months. Every morning they would bring her home to tend her flowers. The first Christmas after my grandfather's death, she decorated a tree in her living room and arranged her special Christmas ornaments. She sat with them and her twinkling lights until it was dark and time to leave again. After the holidays, she gave her furniture to those who wanted it. One January afternoon, she closed her door for the last time.

My mother still drove her to church each day and waited while she lit her candles and prayed. Three years later grandma died and I was happy for her and all her saints.

"Oh, Chan, I don't want to go on with this. It's only making me sad. It's over," I said.

They dressed her in pale gray lace and covered her with tiny roses, pink like her china. They put her in the ground next to my grandfather and we brought flowers until they read her will.

She left me her Bible and her diamond ring; my brothers mementos of my grandfather. She gave the other grandchildren things I can't remember. Two of her children received a small inheritance; the rest letters. My mother was left with a letter.

She threw it away, but it didn't matter. The Bible told me of the dates of my parents' marriage and the birth of a child, with my name and birthdate. However, *that* child was listed as having been born to another of my grandmother's daughters.

It was grandma's way of not letting us forget the price of sinning. My mother, unmarried, had become pregnant and grandma had arranged that I be given to a barren daughter, a good daughter whose heart, according to the ornately written entry, was full of faith and love. I lived with this aunt until I was two years old believing I was hers when my mother, then married, returned to reclaim me.

It was not a time I had remembered, but one that always confused me. Wondering what happened to the hugs and reassurances. Wondering, indeed, if my mother had two separate identities. Building, in my mind, as a child, a space for each. I imagined the good mother locked in the dark green walls of my parents' home. I believed she was waiting patiently for the bad mother, who sat with my brothers on the rose colored couch, to disappear. The memories of that earlier time splattered on the pages of my grandmother's Bible.

Another aunt told me the letter was not a note from their dead mother, but an accounting. My grandmother's way of settling debts. It reminded mother of her sins against God and those against her parents, it thanked her for not interfering with my religious upbringing. It did not forgive my mother for my birth, but wished for mother's continuing decency. It ended by hoping that, one day, they would meet in heaven.

❖❖❖

The light in the office was pale and restful and the city sparkled through yet another plate glass window. "But where will I go, Chan? And who will meet me? Those two old ladies, in their print dresses, standing on a street corner? I know them just as well as my mother and dear grandma."

But, that is not true. I know a grandmother who could not forgive a daughter for having one. I know a mother who wanted a mother's love. And, of course I know a child, who no matter how hard she prayed, never got what she wanted...someone to love her. Finally, I knew myself.

ANNE SCOTT lives in Pasadena, California. She has published several short stories and has recently sold a screenplay entitled *Father's Day*.

WHEN I WAS TWELVE, MY GRANDMOTHER DIED
Margie Lee Gallagher

I took her breakfast that morning
the same as all the others
But mommy had already left
like she said she was going to
A year to the day since poppy died

She always was determined

But I dreamed it was all a mistake
She had only decided to live in the cellar
I was glad to see her there
with her jars of green beans and corn
and peaches and applesauce

She did not say she was glad to see me
but showed me where I had mixed up
the blackberry jelly with the pear honey
and left a whole stack of clean jars
uncovered by the door

She never liked my trifling ways

And I remember that mommy
was once afraid of nobody and no thing
Once I saw her shame a drunk
take his knife, then bandage him up
My sister threw up from the blood

But she cried when the goldenrod bloomed
She hated it, she knew
no matter what she did
winter would come and kill her flowers
the poppies, bachelor buttons, and foxglove

But me, I pick goldenrod
and keep it in a clean mason jar by the door

MARGIE LEE GALLAGHER of Greenville, North Carolina, was raised on a farm in Winchester, Tennessee. She majored in agriculture, obtaining her M.S. and Ph.D. degrees. MARGIE LEE GALLAGHER presently does research on fish at East Carolina University in North Carolina. Writing poetry is her way of keeping in touch with reality.

HIGH STANDARDS
Ruth H. Kuehler

I'm not sure whether I loved my grandmother or just thought her interesting and a source of activities and entertainment. She was too much of a perfectionist to make her loving. She was always kind and patient, but would not stand for any untidiness, poor manners, or a lazy brain. "No idle hands here," and "an idle mind is the devil's workshop," were repeated daily.

In 1915, when I was born, my parents were living in her substantial two-and-one-half story house that she had converted into a downstairs apartment for herself, and an upstairs flat for my mother and father. Josie, the hired girl, had her rooms on the third floor where she had lived since my father and his brother were children. Now she was middle-aged. She ate breakfast and lunch with grandmother, but served her the evening meal. At night Josie ate in the kitchen.

On Mondays the washlady came and both mother and grandmother supervised and pitched in where needed. Their work clothes consisted of black shiny cotton skirts and white shirtwaists over which they wore long, full, bib aprons.

At noon on laundry day they would send Josie to the neighborhood saloon for a bucket of beer, and the four of them, sitting around the kitchen table as equals, ate thick ham sandwiches of rye bread before finishing their work. I would get a sip of beer from each glass as I went around the table listening to their women's talk.

Each day after grandmother awakened from her afternoon nap it was her habit to dress as if she were expecting callers. Even if she did not have an engagement she wore her fine jewelry, and always used lavender cologne. I remember her pleasant fragrance and a special kind of clean smell, and I liked being close to her.

Because it was wartime, and she was offered a fabulous price for the house we lived in, grandmother sold it when I was about four. We moved to a newer neighborhood. The bedrooms in the modern house were all on the second floor and opened into the same hallway. I was put in a small bedroom at the end of the hall overlooking the street. "Now you are a big girl and have a room of your own," mother said, smiling. As she put me to bed she kissed me and closed the door. My parents had disappeared into their own world without me.

I was alarmed to be in a room by myself. I shrieked and sobbed, drawing in my breath. The panic I felt was real, and I can still recreate the hollow, plunging throb in my stomach. I see once more the shadows on the walls turned into ghosts, and the bogeyman of the tales with which my three aunts, not much older than I, had frightened me. I was afraid to tell my mother how her younger sisters terrorized me, while they pretended it was fun.

Mother came into the room later that first night when I couldn't stop crying, and held my head against her soft bosom as I hiccoughed my tears, while I held onto the railing of the iron bed with my sweating hands. The bed had a gate that slipped up and down. It was like a cage. I was helpless. She was just about to lower the gate and lift me out to take me to her room, when grandmother stalked in, hair pulled back severely in a braid, and wearing a dark blue satin robe tied tightly about her slim waist. "Clara, put that child down. Let her cry it out. She has to learn she can't have everything her own way." My mother reluctantly obeyed. I was deserted.

Our next home was a rather cozy flat with a wrought iron range in the kitchen, and a pot-belly stove in the room next to it. Grandmother had a rocker near the stove. It was in this room grandmother and I became close friends. It was the year before I started school.

Grandmother was an insatiable reader and went to literary meetings where they discussed and reviewed books. Often when I asked her to read to me, she read aloud whatever she was reading at the time. The first book I remember hearing, but not understanding at all, was *The Wandering Jew.* Then came *Trilby.* I will never forget my excitement about Svengali and his powers. Adult literature began to appeal to me. In fact from that time on anything in print was fair game.

Peter Rabbit by Beatrice Potter was my favorite, however, and grandmother had me show off to her friends my ability to "read" knowing full well, as I did, that I had memorized the book and knew when to turn the pages from having turned them while she read to me.

Every afternoon I would go to the front door five or six times waiting for the evening paper because in it Uncle Wiggly always had an adventure. But every day I was disappointed because the adventure was so short, and we would read it over and over to make it last. At each reading I hoped something more would happen, but it never did.

She would also hold me on her lap and read the news aloud. I liked being held and listening to her voice, even though I didn't understand the news.

Throughout this period she gradually taught me to read and when adults remarked on it, she said, "Everyone in our family knows how to read before they go to school. How are they going to learn anything in school if they can't read?"

On days when I couldn't play outdoors she had the time to teach me to crochet and to sew doll clothes, to stitch dish towels with cross-stitch design and to carefully hem-stitch handkerchiefs. While I did this she would tell me stories about when my daddy was a little boy, and about my grandfather who had died before I was born.

Because she and my mother didn't always get along, periodically grand-mother would try living by herself or with a widowed friend, but she always came back to us under some new arrangement. I don't think I missed her absences. Children have a way of accepting what is.

Our relationship would change when she lived away from us. During these periods she came once a week for a formal visit to "see her grandchild," she said. She appeared in a black silk dress and drove a black electric car that she steered with a stick. She sat up very high and straight in the car with her chin tilted slightly.

During these visits we didn't read together or embroider. I only leaned against her chair or her knee, and as she caressed my back or smoothed my hair I behaved as to a stranger, while she and my mother talked. Then I would recite a new poem I had learned for grandmother's visit. I carried her cup of coffee to her, and offered her a piece of cake. All under my mother's prompting. I curtsied and felt uneasy with this dressed up visitor who kept her hat on all afternoon.

I was used to her going away, however, because almost every summer she went to Europe with friends to take the baths. She came back with stories about exotic foods, card games and strolling in the garden and streets of Baden Baden.

Then, suddenly, when I was about nine, she came to live with us again. She was evidently ailing. It was whispered she had cancer. The word itself was avoided because it wasn't nice to talk about it. The beautiful tall woman with her regal posture and her hair piled high on her head began to wither.

Despite her decline she made a last effort to continue her round of teas and luncheons. She even gave one at home on her sixtieth birthday, but had to leave her guests and retire to her room, while my mother carried on, and the guests pretended she really seemed to be getting better.

She went to the hospital for a colostomy and here time telescopes in my memory. I think I was about ten when they could not keep the reality of the illness from me any longer. I learned how degrading slow death can be.

Grandmother became a skeleton racked with pain. She begged for the morphine, but the doctor gave firm orders that she must wait four hours between doses.

While she tried to lie quietly and hold off her pain, I read *Sara Crewe, The Secret Garden* and *The Bobbsey Twins* aloud. I think she enjoyed the sound of my voice as our roles were reversed.

After mother gave her the morphine, grandmother would ask me to play something on the piano for her while she sank into the smooth cool sheets and drifted off to sleep. Her favorites were Beethoven's *Moonlight Sonata,* Brahm's *Lullaby,* and a music hall tune, whose first line was, "Tell me pretty maiden are there any more at home like you?" Maybe she had youthful memories of her dancing days when she and her husband enjoyed a show and a supper club afterwards. Old photos suggest she was a fashionably dressed beauty. There's even one of her with an ostrich plume fan and an egret feather in her hair.

I would hear her moan at night and then scream a long wailing cry, and toward the end a nurse came every evening. But even with a pillow over my head I could hear grandmother, and my parents' anxious voices as they talked with the nurse.

I heard the ambulance come. I stood at the door of my room. "We're taking grandmother to the hospital," my mother said. "Lock the door. You'll be safe and try to get some sleep." I looked out the front window. The ambulance moved away. The gas lamps made shadows on the sidewalk.

When my parents came home I was still awake. My father said, "Grandmother passed away." He covered his face with his hands and wept. I don't remember any feeling except relief. I hated the bad smells, the cries of pain. I hated having to put a pillow over my head to try to shut them out. I felt guilty, so I didn't say anything. My mother said, "It's for the best."

In the casket at the wake she looked healthy again. Her skin was fresh and pink and her high cheek bones shone aristocratically. Her hair was thick and full.

After the household had settled back into normalcy I didn't miss her at first. But then gradually as I began to mature, I became aware that although she never actually told me she loved me, she must have been very fond of me to give me so much of her time. I can still hear her say, "A lady never chews gum. A lady never lets anyone know she's upset or uncomfortable, and she never calls attention to anyone's mistakes or bad manners. And, you might as well learn you can't have everything your own way."

I am now a grandmother myself and I am still trying to live up to the standards she set not only for me but for herself as well.

Born is St. Louis, Missouri, RUTH H. KUEHLER has worked in the fields of professional ballet, advertising and physical fitness. Married to a colonel in the army for over forty years, she is now a widow living in San Antonio, Texas. RUTH H. KUEHLER began publishing in 1950 and writing has continued to be the unifying force in her life.

KEEPSAKES
Cherise Wyneken

Cherished cut-glass butter dish,
high, with dome and round,
petaled edges,
bud-like knob at top:
grandma's wedding gift
from long ago
when butter,
churned and shaped
with wooden paddles,
heaped in golden mound,
didn't come in cubes.

Grandma,
round and soft
with golden petaled hair,
churned and shaped by trials.
Motherless at nine,
no time for school or self,
becomes the surrogate,
learning young
that life
fused by tinder mounds of love,
doesn't come pre-packaged
in perfect, die-cut cubes.

Because of geographic separation, CHERISE WYNEKEN of Fort Lauderdale, Florida, must resort to vicarious grandmothering through her children's stories, poems, and devotions appearing in such periodicals as *Aim, Day Care and Early Education, Teachers Interaction, The Home Altar, Touch* and *Wee Wisdom.* She has also written a few adult articles and poems.

THE STRENGTH OF THE CAT
Kathleen M. McNamara

In 1916 my grandmother came to America in a buckboard loaded with dreams, five children and all her possessions. Now those turn-of-the-century immigrant days are fast fading into a new century and new waves of immigrants are reaching American shores. It feels strange to have ties to an era that's portrayed in history books. I've stood with each foot in a different culture; I've celebrated many Thanksgivings with a traditional American turkey dinner alongside huge platters of my grandmother's pasta.

Grandma wasn't like my friends' grandmothers, all soft and round, sweet smelling and merry. Life had made her serious, wiry-thin and strong; so strong that a tug at my wrist when I acted up would oblige me to calm down immediately. When I scraped a knee and needed a hug, I found little comfort in her bony embrace. Besides, a bulky hearing aid battery strapped to her chest always got in the way and banged me on the head or in the face.

We learned a lot about each other one afternoon when I was five years old. My parents had left me with her while they went shopping. I wanted to go with them and I was so angry about being left behind that I wet my pants. I just stood there in her big old garlic-smelling kitchen and let her know what I thought about it all. By the time I came along she'd raised five of her own children and was in the process of helping to raise five of her grandchildren so she took my behavior in stride. That is, until she attempted to remove my panties and I bit her hand, hard! Suddenly my right hand was locked in her vise-grip and the underwear was unceremoniously removed for washing. She didn't scream or make a scene but it was obvious that the bite had hurt more than her hand. I couldn't go out to play because my clothing required the remainder of the afternoon to dry so I had plenty of opportunity to think about my behavior and, by the time my parents returned, I was feeling pretty childish and embarrassed about the whole episode.

Grandma never mentioned the incident to my parents; perhaps because I was the only child of her youngest and favorite son and I looked like her. I'd even been given the Irish equivalent of her name, Catherine. Or maybe she'd seen a version of her younger self standing there in the kitchen that day, defying the world.

Grandma's toughness wasn't all physical. In the days before women were supposed to be able to get on without men, she had to. My grandfather died suddenly of a burst appendix after they'd moved to America from British Columbia. Since two of their daughters were deaf as a result of childhood illnesses and there weren't any special schools to teach them in Canada, grandma had a choice. She could pack up and move back where her brother and friends could lend support or she could stay where she was for her children's sake. She was isolated here and the supply lines of support were growing more tenuous; the rest of her family, her parents and sisters, were still in Italy but she chose to stay.

How difficult it must have been, back then, to live in a small American town where people were unused to tawny-skinned foreigners who spoke broken English. Even I, a second generation Italian watered down with Irish, have felt some of the town's prejudice. The townspeople had already settled in and had obviously forgotten that our country was founded by millions of immigrants.

Despite the cultural differences, in the lean Depression years following her husband's death, she went about the task of raising her children by selling milk and eggs to the neighbors and parceling off sections of the property she and grandpa had acquired. My father said she made sure they never lacked for the necessities, but he and his brother still had to quit school after the tenth grade in order to work and help out. Even though it was hard to provide for her family, life in America was still easier than the first years of her life which were spent picking olives in the most poverty-stricken, hard-scrabble part of southern Italy.

By the time I was born, the hard times were receding memories but my father had presented grandma with new problems; he'd married a divorced woman, an anathema to a pious Catholic. Despite everybody's good intentions, the relationship between my mother and grandma was often rocky. As a result, in my early years, my grandmother was just a white-haired, dressed-in-black matron who smelled like Vicks and gave me rosary beads or a picture of the Pope and a five dollar bill on Christmas and birthdays. When mother and grandma were on good terms, we'd visit grandma as a family. But when they weren't getting along, I was sent over on Sunday afternoons alone with my father for the obligatory visit.

It was always difficult for me to love my grandmother because I felt that would violate a deeper loyalty to my mother. My grandma displayed an unusual sensitivity about my dilemma; every Sunday she'd draw me aside and tactfully ask about my mother. Somehow, after that acknowledgement, it was easier to go on with the dinner and visiting.

My mother, on the other hand, rarely missed the opportunity to criticize my grandmother. It never seemed fair that none of my grandmother's strengths were seen as positive, not even her strong commitment to her faith. When she was angry with me, mother added to my confusion by reminding me that I looked and acted just like my grandmother.

My mother was right in some ways. A few genes skipped a generation and came directly from my grandma to me. Not only did we share similar physical characteristics, the same eyes and forehead, we shared the same crazy passion for order, neatness, and cats. I even inherited her green thumb.

Grandma's biggest limitation wasn't her fault but it shamed me to admit to my friends with the American grandmas that mine couldn't write her own name in her native Italian let alone English. My cousin studied Italian in school and concluded that grandma didn't even speak a grammatically correct Italian! Despite those overwhelming handicaps, she'd managed to sign to my deaf aunts. They'd learned to sign in the English alphabet, but years before American Sign Language added its own variations, she'd been communicating effectively with her daughters in a patois all her own.

Even when grandma wasn't getting along with mother, I always knew there was a place for me in her heart. She'd designated a sign in her special lexicon that stood for me. It was two upward strokes of the fingers from the mouth to the cheek which signified a cat's whiskers; to her I represented "cat", not only her namesake and the first three letters of her name but the animal we both loved best.

When grandma grew older and could no longer hear and her eyesight, as well as her mind, had grown fuzzy, I'd make the cat sign on her cheek so she'd know who had come to visit. She'd smile and nod knowingly. Then she'd reach out and take hold of my arm with that still mighty grip of hers and draw me into her bony arms for a hug.

KATHLEEN M. McNAMARA lives in Milpitas, California. She edits and publishes a quarterly literary magazine, *The Pinehurst Journal*. She's been published in *Runner's World*, *Catholic Digest*, *Cat Fancy* and *Innisfree* and is currently working on a screenplay. When she's not writing or reading manuscripts, she enjoys running and biking.

HOMEMAKER
Cinda Thompson

My grandmother was born to be
My grandmother, surrounded by
Pies, lightly dusted in flour,
Or so I thought until
Relatives told me the story of
How she faced down men
Who came to the door to search
For my grandfather, activist
Coal miner, I stand for
The union, she refrained from saying,
What she did say was simply
My man is not home, meaning
My grandfather hid in the attic,
Meaning armed force would have to
Get past her first
In order to touch a hair
On the head of a single person
In her home, her rolling pin
Off in the kitchen, just an apron
To protect her at the front door,
When as a young lady
I interviewed my grandmother,
Asked her of what in life
Was she most proud,
The older woman answered
Each of my children lived to be
An adult, I try to imagine
A woman who chose to stand
On stone steps in front of guns yet
Kneel at night beside that bed
Racked with both cough and a fever,
She who called me
Her princess on the morning
I was born
And when I walked into
Her arms.

"The story of the coal mines and the families who worked them strikes at something deep and true, the very core of human experience," claims CINDA THOMPSON. The Southern Illinois native, now living in Peoria, has most recently been published in *Cries of the Spirit* (Beacon Press, 1991) and *Looking for Home* (Milkweed Editions, 1990), as well as in numerous other anthologies and periodicals.

HER INTENSITY WAS SLENDER AND SILENT
Joan Payne Kincaid

It wasn't clear
to a child
your life and missing husband
then you came to be mine
I remember being four
in your silent incompleteness.
A dead father when I was five
sent you away
to an aunt for twenty years
cleaning and cooking
your skeleton in dated 1930's
black with white flower repetitions
busy silent as a bird
with a cloth covering its cage.

Mother moved me to your street
where I became an outsider
not your granddaughter
we resigned
grandmothering the others
every meal
mashing mashing
roasting garlic roasts
(up the street fare was spam)
mopping mopping their lives
for a luxury
cup of tea
at 4 p.m. you borrow
their front porch
sometimes with me
until pneumonia silence.

Serve two generations
my nana they took
from me and never knew
you were there.

JOAN PAYNE KINCAID of Sea Cliff, New York, is an internationally published poet who has written most of her life. She gives frequent readings and occasionally hosts the radio program *Sounds of Poetry* for the Long Island Poetry Collective. Tea with Mary Landrigan Kennedy at 4 p.m. represented treasured moments of love during her childhood.

COTTON BALLS AND MYSTICISM
Wayt Hamill

Looking at Grandma Belle was like peacefully looking at the ages of all knowledge. I loved her snow white hair and her round, flat Indian face with the broad nose. I loved her smooth skin with fewer wrinkles than all her daughters combined. But, most of all, I loved her eyes.

Those large, brown eyes could be as soft as cow eyes as she listened with undivided attention to a young granddaughter prattle on about whatever happened to be important in her life at the moment. Her eyes could flash fire and ice in displeasure as when Uncle Tommy dropped my new house slipper down the outhouse hole or they could reflect the magnified sorrow of the universe as they did when Aunt Janie took her own life.

Throughout childhood I would hurry home from school each day to tell Grandma Belle about my day. Sharing with her was as vital and natural to me as breathing. Small and large lessons were quietly, gently imparted to me on these occasions without preaching and without my knowledge.

In elementary school years seemed to flow quite uneventfully. But, in fourth grade a new girl moved to our town and was in my class. Excited, I ran home to tell Grandma Belle. In a torrent of words I described how she looked and what she wore. When my stream of enthusiasm ran down to a trickle, grandma asked if I had been kind to her. I felt that I hadn't been unkind to her and stated the same. Grandma said that wasn't the same as purposely being kind.

It was that day that she taught me about keeping cotton balls on my feet. She told me that I was actually stepping into the life of each new person I met. She paused there to let the serious implications of that fact sink in. She then said that this was a grave responsibility. Having stepped into a life, no matter how temporarily, I should always imagine having cotton balls on the bottom of my feet so I would tread softly and lightly in that life. If I always thought of the cotton balls when I met someone new, I would be reminded not to leave that life damaged when either of us walked on.

So it was with this level of close communication we had built over the years that I hit adolescence. In my usual fashion I hurried home one day to tell grandma the hottest gossip to hit our school... a female classmate was doing IT.

Grandma Belle's eyes flashed. Her thin lips formed a straight line of raging disapproval. She bellowed at me, "IT is called sex or sexual intercourse! Have YOU engaged in sexual intercourse?"

Shocked, I shrank back, wide-eyed and terrified. She had never spoken to me in that tone. All I could do was timidly shake my head.

146

"Well," she said, "all the more reason you will say no more about this young woman because you don't understand what you are talking about!"

She proceeded to lecture me. The words may not be exactly as she spoke them, but the substance, burned into my memory forever, was something like this: All young women should refrain from sexual intercourse until they marry. However, someday you will understand that once you begin to have sex you never want to do without it again. Sex becomes a craving. Under the right circumstances, with someone you care for deeply, it is the most wonderful experience you will ever have. God knew what he was doing when he designed our bodies, the fit is perfect, and the sexual act is one of the few mystical experiences in life that ordinary people ever have. The very best part about the experience is that you can be mystical like that over and over again until the moment you die.

She must have known the question forming in my mind as I stared at her for she smiled, her large brown eyes dancing as she chuckled, "Yes, I still partake of my share of mysticism."

These lessons were offered many years ago, but if I could be granted one wish today, it would be the opportunity to sit once more on the floor at the feet of Grandma Belle and look up into those attentive, sparkling eyes. I long to tell her how my life is going, how this particular day is going. I long to tell her that I am now the grandmother. I long to see the twinkle in her eyes as I tell her I have tried very hard to wear cotton balls on my feet and that, yes, I still partake of my share of mysticism, too.

WAYT HAMILL, a writer and social worker, received her M.S.W. cum laude from the University of Washington. She lives in Seattle, Washington, and in Guadalajara whenever she can get away. She and her husband, John, have seven mystical children and five cotton-ball-trained grandchildren.

A SUDDEN SENSE OF HER

GRANDMA BESSIE
Barbara Foster

Decades I've worn your amethyst
   ring
Matriarch conveniently invisible
   to your children
Heirlooms, rare gems of a skimpy
   life
Decorate my hands, unknown
   to the steam press

Five babes and a dead
   husband
Sentenced you to a tailor
   shop
Until the kids grew up
And you became the child

Guilty of being old, poor
Stored in the spare bedroom
No one saw you laugh
   or weep
A specter hidden in shadow

Summers in Atlantic City
Bar Mitzvahs, a cheap permanent
At family affairs, they pushed
   your tattered bulk
In the corner like a second-
   hand sofa

Why didn't you speak the poems
You wrote down in secret
Passed on to my obedient
   mother
To hide behind Jewish Congress
   smiles?

It happened, a foolish cousin
Revealed your furtive fate
Explained why images infect
   my reality
Why I dream in metaphors

Bessie the ignored, become
  my muse
To resurrect the songs entombed
Within both women, martyred
On duty's thankless pyre

Give me the ammunition
To avenge your restless ghost
And wrench my own salvation
From the evasive cosmic cheat.

BARBARA FOSTER, Assistant Professor at City University of New York, has been published widely in poetry journals and anthologies in the U.S., Canada, Australia and Great Britain. While poetry is her passion, she is also the author of *Forbidden Journey: The Life of Alexandra David-Neel* (Harper & Row, 1987).

CODA
Robin Dellabough

They are playing Stravinsky at the Hollywood Bowl
when notes pierce through the skin of years.

Suddenly I am seven, climbing narrow stairs to my grandmother's.
She wears a flowered dress, belted with a bow.
Her bare wrinkled arms flutter as she bends toward me.
More flowers, then the musty scent of heavy furniture
crowded into small rooms. The tall clock beats out time.
She pulls down a scrapbook: dance cards, pressed flowers,
yellow clippings of her concerts.
Now she plays only for me,
her own compositions, simple and sweet,
not at all like this capriccio for piano
I hear in the distance.
She cooks my meat with elusive spices I have not tasted since.
Then I sink into down and linen, dream without memory.

I wake knowing she has been here.
That long trip from Seattle to Mexico to Michigan
where they waited out the Depression—
surely she came for the music one night,
saw the white curves over the stage,
let herself drift wistfully,
forgetting her two little boys, her out-of-work husband,
the audience that would not hear her play.

ROBIN DELLABOUGH is a poet, writer and editor. Her work has appeared in small literary journals such as *Blue Unicorn*, *Footworks*, *Maryland Poetry Review*, *Mildred*, *Negative Capability*, *The Doula* and *Recovery*. She has a master's degree in journalism and co-authored the national bestseller, *50 Simple Things You Can Do to Save the Earth*. She recently moved from Berkeley, California, to Irvington-on-Hudson, New York, where she lives with her husband and two young children.

AMATEURS
Denise Low

I dip the brush into the ice tea glass
and water shimmies phthalo blue.
Tap, tap it on the side to knock off
drops before the plunge
onto wide open white.
Mark off grids of meaning—
clouds and hills maybe—
if the color will hold still long enough
but most beautiful is
sun shining through the water glass.

This clumsy landscape wouldn't fool the dog
but I remember my grandmother
painting vases and birds of paradise
I could just make out.
her crimson blurred into enormous peonies
larger than planned, out of control
but dear to her, like memories.
Her ordered life of church choir,
ladies clubs, and gardens thinned out
like background wash as her eyesight dimmed,
yet still she watercolored flowers.

Like her I mix liquid and muddy pigment
into something formless but sun-charged.

DENISE LOW of Lawrence, Kansas, has published several books of poetry and chapbooks. She received an M.F.A. in creative writing from Wichita State and an M.A. in English from Kansas University. She teaches English and creative writing at Haskell Indian Junior College. She has received the Kansas Arts Commission Fellowship for literature, a Roberts Foundation Award, *Kansas Quarterly* Seaver Awards, and fellowships from the National Endowment for the Humanities. Her grandmother, Carrie Dotson, wrote poetry and participated in literary clubs.

BECOME YOUR BUBBE
Elaine Starkman

bring yourself back
to her present

feel as she feels
know her world

your feet
under her earth

stirring soup
bearing babies

daring/
     Amerika?

your body moves
to her rhythm

simple/separate
fearful of cossacks

who make you
into peasant/usurer

your heart takes
pleasure in her pleasures

lets out sorrow
in her sorrow

your stomach fills
with borscht/potatoes

warmth and tears
trickle down her throat

that opens you
to ideas

gives you good English
high cheek bones/light hair

a slippery mind
that moves in/out of cultures

trying to guard/discard
what history it wants to learn

Both the prose and the poetry of ELAINE STARKMAN have been published exten-
sively. Long a teacher of writing, she has recently edited *Without a Single Answer:
Poems on Contemporary Israel* (Magnes Museum, Berkeley, 1990). The Walnut Creek,
California resident has just herself become a grandma.

WHERE MY GRANDMOTHER LAUGHS
Joanna M. Weston

Grandmother
is a strange being
of short breath
and big insult
impoverished sight
rich vision
a conundrum of tall delight
and slim modernity
who impales my teen insight
on a spike
of tart wisdom

her questions are
twice asked
comments quadruple
given
and I don't
understand but
I reply

she finds me under
the willow tree
cave where no one
but me can hide in falling
shadows down green
in sunlight

this is where
my grandmother lives
under the rustling
laughter of trees

JOANNA M. WESTON, currently of Shawnigan Lake, British Columbia, was born in England but has lived in Canada since 1958. She and her husband, Robert, have three sons—Andrew, Jon and Mark—as well as a ginger cat named Fred. Her work has been published in Canada, the United Kingdom and in the United States since 1983.

THE JEWEL
Rona Spalten

It was like this once a month, on the visits: the dark room—the blinds drawn so the fabric of the furniture wouldn't fade—my grandmother moaning as if softly singing a lullaby and I, alert to everything, soaking in the sights and medicinal smells of my pathetic looking grandmother, frightened that later when my grandmother took me into the bedroom and offered me a jewel, I'd do the wrong thing and take it, adding it to the collection I kept hidden from my mother.

My mother claimed that my grandmother's toenails were like claws. That they were abnormally thick, crusty, and disgusting; nobody, nobody else would want to cut them. She was the only one willing to take care of these things. She knelt at my grandmother's feet, cradling one foot after the other in her lap, her face screwed up distastefully, muttering, "Why am I doing this? You never did anything for me. You never even kept the house clean for us."

Clip, clip. Through such thickness. Clip, clip. Dried out old nails falling to the floor. In the quiet. While I watched and waited, grandmother moaned, and the nails fell in the musty, deathlike room.

Then it was over and my mother got up. "I'm going to make lunch. I brought bread and cake from the baker's, meat from the butcher. Especially for you, mother." She went into the kitchen, and I was left with my grandmother.

Now my grandmother didn't seem sick. Now my grandmother jumped up, her eyes bright, reaching out her crooked, decaying fingers, putting them on my thin arm, which was like a new branch sprouting from an old tree. "Come," grandmother said. "I have something for you."

I tried to still myself. This happened every time I came, and I didn't understand why my mother and my grandmother were so opposed, why my mother insisted on doing and doing, while my grandmother insisted on moaning and dreaming over her jewels.

The bedroom was bright with sunlight streaming in the open window. In the backyard, a small tree was sprouting its first green children, and the dark earth was waiting for a garden. Grandmother went to stand in front of the dresser.

The jewels were kept in a wood box in the top drawer. Every time I came to visit, my grandmother took out the jewels, poured them on the bed. Each jewel had a memory and my grandmother told me the memories one at a time. My mother had told me many times how angry she was that her mother had never learned English properly and was difficult to understand—she could never bring friends home when she was a child in fear that they'd make fun of grandmother—but I delighted in my grandmother's foreignness and felt I could understand her perfectly. I listened to the rhythm of my grandmother's speech, filling in her supposed meanings for the foreign words, and in this way my grandmother told me of her first dance, her first date, a party she went to when she was young—still in Russia—of meeting her husband, of her marriage, special moments after, of arriving in America, of being on the boat and staring at the ocean. "In the ocean," she said, "I stared so many days, and I saw how the waters reflected the rise and fall of the moon, and I kept waiting and looking and then I saw that the ocean reflected me too. There I was: arriving in a new country with rosy cheeks and excited eyes."

Sometimes my mother came to the doorway and caught us conspiring this way. She would stand with her hands on her hips. "Put away your junk, mother," she said, "I don't want you to fill Esther's head with garbage. She has trouble enough doing what she's supposed to. She's always daydreaming."

"Your mother," grandmother said, "goes and goes and does and does, but she never considers who she is. It is too bad she never stops to treasure anything or make anything special. She thinks that I am moaning because I am sick and that is true. Soon I will die, but I am also calling. I am calling and wooing out my memories, all the special moments, all the moments when dreams met with life and came true."

I picked up a red rhinestone set in a gold daisy flower and pressed it to my chest, staring at it in the mirror. I thought of my mother's sharp impatient fingers on my arms as she rushed me along, and the day I sat by her ironing board angry that she'd stopped me from going off with older children, trying to read to her some little poem I'd written and having her tell me to please be quiet. In the jewel I saw myself as someone different, a future self perhaps, a radiant happy blooming woman, a person my mother wouldn't recognize, the way my grandmother must have seen herself reflected in the ocean. And there was my grandmother, too, in the mirror over the oak dresser, with her red kerchief tied around her white hair. She wasn't moaning now but looked happy and content, beckoning me, calling me out to her ocean of dreams. I didn't want to end up like her, alone, moaning over jewels and memories, but I couldn't resist what she offered either. I'd hide the jewels amongst my underwear in a lingerie bag I'd stolen from my mother, and at night, special moments, I'd take them out, one by one, and see myself dancing, dancing round and round, the way my grandmother had danced, and I'd dream, even if I had to go against my mother. So I turned, displaying the jewel pressed to my chest and said, "Yes, grandmother, I'll take it. I'll take this one."

RONA SPALTEN of Oakland, California, obtained an M.A. in creative writing from Sonoma State University. She teaches adults in such diverse areas as ESL, creative writing and bodywork. Additionally, as a hypnotherapist, she works with people on creativity and health issues.

LOOSE PHOTOGRAPH
Robin Greene

My grandmother sprawls in tall grass
at seventeen: Betty, Divine Corners

the photograph border reads; stockings
rolled down below her knees, Victorian
dress hiked up as high as the wildflowers

around her. Girl, woman, waist-long
hair parted forward over covered breasts,

she turns her face from the camera,
one hand clinging to her dress hem,
the other caught opening around

the stem of an unpicked daisy.
Old photograph, discovered loose among

the pasted others as I sort through familiar
and unfamiliar faces in a family album.
Grandmother, dead now for fifteen years,

once neither a mother nor a wife,
I take your photograph into the kitchen
for better light, hold you up and stare—

not to understand anything certain
or profound, but only to look at you again.

ROBIN GREENE holds an M.A. in English and an M.F.A. in writing. She recently published a collection of poetry entitled *Memories of the Light* and is currently working on a book concerning women's birthing experiences. ROBIN GREENE teaches part-time at Methodist College in Fayetteville, North Carolina, and is married with two children.

SHADOWY CORNERS
Marilyn Reynolds

I wish I could remember more of my grandmother from those long ago childhood days. The old family Bible tells me she was born June 7, 1881, and died June 13, 1956. I know that she and her husband came to California from Ohio in 1906, but such information seems impersonal and I search the dark recesses of young memory for more.

Sometimes I can hear her voice, from the shadowy corners of my cluttered mind, telling me of her life. She would tell me of her husband, the grandfather I never knew. "Elmer was great fun," she would say. "He was always laughing about something. He died laughing, you know," she would say with a smile. And hearing this story, each time, I would long for my always laughing grandfather.

There was a time when she was out in the fields of the old Ohio farm, and she felt something move beneath her bare foot. A snake! Every time she told me that story, I felt the old Ohio snake beneath my young California foot, and my toes writhed inside my shoes.

When I was so young that I sat on floors instead of furniture, I liked to feel the floor shake when she walked across the room with her heavy step. When I was old enough to be trusted not to put coins in my mouth, she let me wash pennies and showed me how to shine them on the rug. She bought peppermint sticks and taught me how to use them as straws for my water at lunch time.

My grandmother liked dogs, and she gardened. I would watch as she worked in her garden, sweat rolling in big drops down her cheeks. Sometimes a drop would slowly work its way to the end of her nose, then plop ceremoniously into the dirt below. I was envious and wished I could sweat like she did. I asked her to teach me, but she told me she couldn't do that. My mother was forever and always telling me I was too young to do something, or too young to understand. I wondered if my grandmother felt that way about me and the sweating knowledge. She had never given me the "too young" line, so I couldn't be sure.

She played croquet and camped out at Huntington Beach. In the springtime, she drove me out to the desert, so I could see carpets of wildflowers in bloom. Once we went to Banning to pick cherries. Her knees were ticklish and sometimes she would get nosebleeds. (Nosebleeds were something else I wished I could imitate, but couldn't.) The can of Pet milk that she always kept handy for her coffee gave me my first intimation of infinity, with the picture of the cow, within the picture of the cow, within the picture of the cow, within the...

On the high chest in her bedroom, there was a tiny house with a little boy figure and a little girl figure on some kind of swivel. When the boy was out, it meant there would be rain, and when the girl was out it meant fair weather. The trick to remembering which figure meant nice weather, she said, was to remember that girls were nicer than boys.

I loved the food at granny's house. Her potato salad, with hot bacon, hard boiled eggs, homemade mayonnaise and added bacon grease would today be considered lethal by the anti-cholesterol forces. Still, my mouth waters at the memory.

My favorite meal, which she always fixed for me on the first night of a weekend stay, was fried pork chops, fried potatoes, cottage cheese and tomatoes, served with sugar sprinkled generously over each item. She baked angel food cakes for me on each of my first fifteen birthdays, until her aging brain could no longer distinguish between egg shells and flour and her days in the kitchen ended.

On Christmas mornings, hers were the gifts I opened first. She gave me a watch when my parents thought I was much too young to take care of it, and cowboy paraphernalia when my parents thought I should be playing with baby dolls.

She told me how her husband Elmer, the one who laughed so much he died, had first come to their farm to visit her sister Cora. While he was courting Cora in the parlor, my grandmother took his coat from the stand in the hallway and sewed up all of the pockets with tiny, tight stitches. When he got on the trolley for the last leg of his journey home, he couldn't get his money from his coat pocket and was kicked off the trolley. After that, he quit courting Cora and fell in love with granny.

Sundays she would often take me, by bus, from her little house in Monterey Park, over to the Country Church of Hollywood. It was a big white church, made of wood, and it had a steeple and a gospel quartet. The harmonies and sentiment of *What a Friend We Have in Jesus,* and *On the Jericho Road,* were pleasing to my ear, and I first learned to recognize certain words while I followed along with my grandmother in the hymnal.

She could touch her hands flat on the floor without bending her knees. Before I knew her, she said, she used to get bad headaches. But then she had her hair cut and stopped filling her head full of hair pins, and the headaches stopped. She told me people shouldn't talk bad about Jews because Jesus was a Jew, and she worried about the boys, who looked like men to me, going off to fight the war.

Granny died when she was seventy-five and I was twenty-one and by that time neither of us knew the other anymore. By then, the only trips she took to see the wildflowers or pick cherries came unpredictably to her mind, back and forth, past times and other past times, all while she was sitting in a chair, gazing out the window of a San Gabriel rest home.

I wish I could remember more of her from those long ago days, but then that's probably what she wished about me the last time I saw her sitting in the chair, face toward the window. I would like to have an evening with her, over sugared food and peppermint stick water, to talk woman to woman about her life. And I would like to let her know that I often think of her on those occasions when grown up sweat drips from my face, and that at least once every summer I mix bacon grease into my potato salad.

MARILYN REYNOLDS is a writer and teacher whose essays have appeared in newspapers nationwide. She is the author of a young adult novel, *Telling*, published by Peace Ventures Press, and *Grace* an as yet unpublished mainstream novel. She and her husband, Michael, live in Altadena, California.

HER SILENCE
Ruth Daigon

Swollen with the shapes and sounds
of all her children,
how did she shrink so quickly?

What happened to her hair
that she must keep it
hidden underneath her kerchief
or a wig? Did she lose it
from a childhood illness
or tear it by the roots
when her oldest drowned?

How hard it was to pray
when she had no one to pray with.
Her husband left her far behind
somewhere in the shtetl along
with prayer shawl and beard.
Das Kapital gave him new
disguises and all her sons and
daughters paraded off with him.

Not one grand child
volunteered to carry home
her Bible from the synagogue
unless a fist directed him.

No one listened to her stories
from the other side except
a few old ladies who had
heard them all before and
wouldn't listen anyway, they
had their own stories waiting.

One by one the old shapes
grew dim and disappeared.
She could no longer thread her needle,
or hear the front door slam.

I move across the continent
back to heavy snows and
the warm kitchen where her sighs
fall from every crack
in the plaster, covering me
with thin layers of sound
until I become her shadow,
smelling of strange earth,
smelling of places she has
been and gone from and I will
never know except I understand
the language of her silence now.

RUTH DAIGON of Mill Valley, California, is editor of *Poets On:* She was performing poet for The Connecticut Commission on the Arts and has given readings throughout the United States, Canada, England and Israel where her work has been extensively published. RUTH DAIGON is a former soprano with the New York Pro Musica.

THE OLD COUNTRY
Rosemund Handler

She was from the old country and her attitude to dating was, "Vy go out mit von ven you can go mit four?" I would shake my head and smile, partly amused but mostly impatient. "Gran, nobody dates like that anymore—one guy at a time is enough to cope with." She'd look sceptical and pitying—so many lost opportunities.

She was never one to let an opportunity slip by and before I would go out she'd call out, "And don't make yourself cheap!" This latter condition embraced a spectrum of behavior and dress that might range from a warm greeting (too much of a come-on) to a sleeveless blouse (displaying the goods too soon—a poor strategy for entrapment).

Heaven forbid that the unwary date for the evening should not present himself—he was garbage for all eternity. But make the right kind of eye contact with her—she was an incorrigible flirt—and you won her heart. Most of my dates failed to recognize her influence and lost a golden opportunity, usually with me as well as my grandmother!

She ruled her daughters with a rod of iron. Even at a ripe old age her fierce eyes and turned-down mouth signaled dire disapproval, causing them to drop like nine pins. It just was not worth getting on the wrong side of her; she'd been too often proven uncannily close to the bone.

She was very suspicious of anyone my mother used to date and even at the age of twenty-five my mom would have to be back at a set time. Gran would not go to bed until she knew her daughter was home. On one occasion my mother was escorted to the door by her date, a man my grandmother had met on several occasions. They kissed at the door and my mother claims now that while she could see nothing there was an almost palpable presence—a malevolent one— and the young man withdrew hastily.

My mother turned her key in the lock and opened the door. My grandmother sprang on her in a fury and slapped her twice painfully across the face. Bewildered, my mother confronted her. "What have I done wrong?"

Apparently kissing at the front door was tantamount to having sex on the patio—taboo. Any demonstrations of affection—and these should be minimal— should be behind closed doors, where the neighbors had no hope of a view. My mother never thought to question her own mother's voyeurism.

The man I married also had to win her over before he felt truly accepted as a member of the family and it happened at a rather inappropriate time. My cousin had been killed in a tragic auto accident within days after my fiance and I had become engaged. At the prayers my fiance and I were separated in the crowd and the only face he recognized was that of my grandmother. Their eyes locked and my husband smiled. She looked taken aback and then smiled coyly and winked. Despite the somber occasion, she could never resist the right kind of male attention.

When she died my mother and her sisters felt they'd lost a limb, so much a part of them was her hectoring, caring presence.

I pass someone on the street sometimes who has something of her in her eyes and I smile because wherever she is, part of her is still here, alive in me.

ROSEMUND HANDLER migrated to Los Angeles from South Africa in 1988. She has settled well but has come to appreciate the sense of "otherness" experienced by her Russian grandparents in Africa. It seems she, too, was born to wander—part of an ancient bloodline driven by a restless compulsion to move when the environment becomes hostile. ROSEMUND HANDLER works full time with her husband and writes when she can.

OF TIME AND PLACE
Chalise Miner

Eighty-nine years ago you entered the world,
Obedient to the rigors of a manila colored childhood.
Young ladies, without asking questions,
Wore long cotton stockings and sensible shoes.
Some future lay ahead, as far as you could walk,
If you chanced to glimpse it.
More commonly, it entwined with a farm down the road,
Land and families blending, like yellow-gold hay bales
Left in the sun to serve the world.
Chaperoned courtships.
Youthful unions cradling young.
The courage to bake for farm hands ten pies today
And rise tomorrow to bake ten more,
Has brought you to this mechanical bed, a call bell
And stiff ironed sheets.
I watch you sleep,
Certain each breath will take you away from me,
Knowing, when it does, it will be before I've grasped your will,
Understanding less how you lived than why you refuse to die.

CHALISE MINER writes from her home in Kansas City. She is married and the mother of three. Her poems, articles and stories have appeared in *St. Anthony Messenger*, *Kansas City Parent* and *Sun Magazine*. This poem won Honorable Mention in the 1990 Kansas State Poetry Contest.

IN MEMORY OF ROSE
Jackie Fox

So much hardness and softness
in my grandma!
She long retained the shyness
of certain children.
Half a glass of wine
made her blush like a schoolgirl.
In my mind I can see her
perched on her kitchen stool,
one of the rare times
she told girlhood stories.

She remembered the discomfort
of reciting in class—
the one-room schoolhouse
full of immigrant children.
"'Rosa Dachtler,' the teacher would say,"
she recalled in a lilting singsong,
accenting the first syllables
of each word.
Her face grew red just from remembrance,
and she clapped her hands in delight
like any child.

Yet she held herself rigid
the first time my grown father hugged her.
It was after his first hug
from his daughter, also grown.
Even she never would have done it
had she not moved so far away from home.

The language of touch,
so foreign to my family,
caused my grandmother to stiffen
like the starched shirts
of the young boys in the country school.
I can't remember if she ever hugged
my father back.

Even now, if I were to see her,
it would be in the poorest taste
to speak of affection.
But the ivory-colored afghan
she sent at Christmas
whispers love from the rocker
each time I pass.

JACKIE FOX lives and writes in Lincoln, Nebraska. She is a senior writer for *PC Today* and an after-hours poet. Her poems have appeared in *Rolling Stone, Plainswoman* and *Whole Notes*.

GERANIUMS
Meleta Murdock Baker

There were always flowers at my grandma's,
even in winter, even in that dirty city block.
She'd take sooty black soil from her
tiny back yard
and make those plants grow.
Her place smelled of geraniums and oil paints—
not sweet, but true and familiar.
I was alarmed when she started
collecting those awful plastic bouquets,
the colors wrong for any flower:
too-bright orange that faded to pink
then gathered dust in the sunlight.
My childish inspection revealed
careless manufacture—
nothing like the magic she worked
with tiny buds or velvety violets.
Gradually, shame pierced my selfish ignorance,
and my anger (once thrown at her newly blurred
paintings) jumped back on myself
and burned.
Even now, thirty years later,
the scent of geraniums brings back
my private guilt of not seeing sooner
that she was eighty-eight years old and
going blind.

MELETA MURDOCK BAKER lives in Lebanon, Maine, with her husband, daughter, and several dozen wild birds. A teacher at Wells High School, she is advisor to its literary magazine, *Writers' Bloc*. She is the co-founder of the Gully Oven Folkschool and a founding member of the Salmon Falls Friends of Music. Her quilt is incomplete and her piano is dusty, but her poetry has been published in the anthology *If I Had a Hammer: Women's Work* and in various magazines.

MARY HYNES REMEMBERED
Joyce McMillin Everett

Grandma Mary...
A sudden sense of her
Haunts my steps
Across the lawn
I stop
Arms full of laundry
How strange
To feel her presence
In my yard
The air is full
Of good smells tonight
Clean laundry
New-mown grass
Flowers
I breathe deeply
Step back forty years
Across half a continent
To stand
Tiny hand in hers
By a birdbath
Where petunias bloom:

"They're no good for cutting, child,
 but I like their smell at night
 When the work's all done."

JOYCE McMILLIN EVERETT was born in Waterloo, Iowa, grew up in Endicott, New York, and currently lives in Hampton Bays, New York, with her husband James. She apportions creative energy to writing desk, pottery studio and flower gardens with frequent time out for family and friends. Her work has appeared in such diverse publications as *Lilith*, *Reader's Digest* and *The Anvil's Ring*.

AFTER THE STROKE
Geraldine Zeigler

Grandmother rolls the wheelchair up
so close it bumps my shins the way
edges of boxes used to do
when I was a child and had to
ride on a stool in the back of
my father's delivery van.
She gestures, tries to force words from
a silent throat, nodding, smiling
at what I say, gentle as a
bronze Buddha.

She reminds me of the well with
the broken windlass that's in the
backyard of her home. The water
is still there with nothing to
bring it up.

GERALDINE ZEIGLER of Pulaski, Tennessee, is a retired teacher. In the past three years she has had over one hundred poems published in various magazines including *Archer, Alura, Old Hickory Review, Word and Image* and *Riverrun.* Recently her chapbook, *Women through the Fog* was published by *The Plowman.*

THE GAME
Sarah Singer

I can see her still,
Hands groping for the key
To wind the clock
Upon the mantelpiece.
It had become a ritual
Played out in pantomime
For her, for me.
I would watch her face
As she listened for the click
That warned the spring was tight;
Mine a child's delight
In whir and beat and chime.

One day I came
To find her still abed;
Told me I must wind the clock,
Made a game of it.
I stood upon a chair
And turned the key
Until she cried: "Enough!"
Not yet aware
Of dooms, I heard her cough.
Mother brought her tea.

Grandma died when I was nine.
Too soon adept,
I wound the clock and wept,
Perceived at last
What striking clocks define.

SARAH SINGER of Seattle, Washington, has recently been awarded prizes by The Washington Poets Association, the Seattle branch of The National League of American Penwomen, and the Portland branch of The Penwomen. Her third book, entitled *The Gathering,* was published in 1991.

THE MUCH OF HER
Susan Brunn-Puett

The much of her stays within my days.
Like gift-wrapped picnics
basketed for indoor spreads,
mocking the rain, she prevails.

The connection shared but unexamined then,
need never be.
About her role, there is
no confusion now.

Her mortality has made
me less afraid of mine.

SUSAN BRUNN-PUETT of Coconut Grove, Florida, is a counselor for young children whose parents are being treated for chemical addiction. In that role, she uses poetry as a tool to encourage the expression of feelings. Her poetry has most recently appeared in *The South Florida Poetry Review.*

MISSOURI TWILIGHT
Lynn Buck

This week we are visiting Grandmother Crow, my favorite person. She lives in Fredericktown, my favorite place in the world. It's a little town in the Ozarks, about a hundred miles from where we live. Supper is over now, and the dishes are done, and we are sitting on the front porch, our family—the way we do just about every evening. Aunt Mabel and Aunt Emma have walked over from their little white house that we can see behind the rail fence across the pasture.

The air is breezy, beginning to cool off now from the heat of the day. The delicate aroma of grandmother's honeysuckle hedge floats about us. I take a long deep breath, delighting in its savory sweetness. I sit here on the porch steps, leaning against one of the front pillars, listening to the sounds of the grown-ups' voices blending with the rise and fall of cicadas signaling the approaching darkness. Mother and Aunt Mabel are sitting on the swing. Each time they move their feet, it jiggles and its rusty chains grate against the ceiling hooks making a loud creeeeeek-craaaaaak. I've always liked that sound. Aunt Emma is in the little bentwood rocker—it's her favorite—and she rocks as briskly as she talks, sort of keeping time to the words. Father is tilted back against the wall in the old ladderback chair. Mother keeps warning him he's either going to break the chair or his back—or maybe both—but he does it anyway. Folks say he and I have the same stubborn streak in us.

Grandmother is in her big wicker rocker. It scrapes softly against the floor as she rocks slowly back and forth. She must be pretty old—she has so many wrinkles on her face. But they're beautiful wrinkles—she wouldn't look right without them. She has smiley blue eyes the color of cornflowers that crinkle up at the corners making still more wrinkles when she laughs. I like to hear her laugh, starting with a low soft chuckle deep in her throat, then growing louder and heartier until her whole body seems to be laughing.

The dusky air is growing chillier, and I pull my skirt down over my legs, hugging my knees against my chest. "Don't you need a sweater, Martha Lynn?" mother asks. "You mustn't catch cold."

I don't want to break the spell. "I'm fine," I say. Everyone looks shadowy and mysterious, gray silhouettes in the dim twilight. And now the first katydid of the evening begins its relentless call. We don't have them at home—only here at grandmother's. "Katy-did," it says over and over, "Katy-did, katy-did," and then a distant answer, "Katy-didn't," then "Katy-did, katy-didn't" in rapid succession. As twilight deepens, the whippoorwills add their mournful voices. We don't have them at home either. Mother says it's because we're too close to the city. We don't have enough woods where we live. And then in the distance I hear the eerie call of a screech owl. It sends shivers through me.

This is a sad time of day when the sun disappears. A lonesome feeling comes over me, and I go over to grandmother and climb up on her lap. She has the softest most comfortable lap in the whole world. That's because she's so nice and plump. I feel awfully sorry for everyone who has skinny grandmothers with skinny bony laps. I can't possibly imagine sitting on any such laps. Grandmother hugs me close against her large soft bosom, sheltering me from the night sounds. She rubs my arms, saying, "My sakes, you've got goose bumps!"

"I'm not cold now," I say.

She hoists me up a little more on her lap. "Gracious, child," she says with a laugh, "you'll soon be too big for my lap! See there—your feet about touch the floor."

"I'm *never* going to be too big for your lap, grandmother," I whisper. "And you're never going to die." I snuggle a little closer.

Grandmother kisses me on the back of my neck. "Children have to grow up," she says, "and everybody has to die eventually." The wooden rockers of her chair press against the worn floorboards, squeaking faintly.

"Not me," I say. The shadows are darkening. I shiver again, and grandmother tightens her embrace. Enveloped by the wispy fragrance of her lavender perfume, I can hear the steady rhythmic thump of her heart and feel the vibrations of her voice as she resumes her conversations with the others. I relax to the gentle motion of the rocking chair. A soothing sense of oneness with this calm quiet little universe flows through me—the rise and fall of grandmother's breasts, the strong heartbeat, the voices blurred in the background, the creaking of the swing, the katydids, the whippoorwills, my own breathing in unison with grandmother's.

Now we catch sight of the faint glimmer of the first star of the evening. "Star light, star bright," I chant, "first star I see tonight…"

"Make a wish," grandmother says, "and if you don't look at that star again, it will come true."

And then mother says, "I think it's time for all little girls to be in bed." It's that special firm tone of voice she uses at bedtime.

"Can't I stay just a little longer?" I ask. She remains silent. "Please," I beg, "just this once." I hold my breath.

"Well, a few more minutes," she says.

Savoring these precious moments of borrowed time, I close my eyes and make my wish. "Let us stay this way forever," I say to the star. I yearn to remain safe and secure on this generous lap, protected from the night and the shadowy darkness forever and ever. But I know the wish cannot come true—even if I don't look at the star again.

LYNN BUCK of Hampton Bays, New York, is Missourian by birth and disposition. Her work has appeared in many national journals and anthologies including *Poets for Africa* and *The Tie that Binds*. She has published a volume of poems, *Autumn Fires* and has completed a novel tentatively titled *Antiques are Rarely Perfect*.

GRANDMA, I TOO AM A GRANDMA
Joanne Seltzer

How wise I have become
nearly as wise as you
and at least as crazy.

You are my role model
the singer of sweet songs
no matter how off-key.

Skin of wax, hair of silk
legs of polished lumber
hand veins of blue ribbon

you were the crone, hag, witch
that folklore is made of.
Now you are my sister.

REQUIEM
Joanne Seltzer

I.
Grandmother Fanny,
the paranoia

I've seen in myself
and in your mother,

must go back as far
as the first mother,

Eve of the apple—
Eve whose name means life.

II.
Two of my daughters
have produced babies

that carry our genes
into the future.

III.
I resemble you,
at least in profile,

now my hair has grayed
and my skin wrinkled

and my eyes grown dim
from too much vision.

We're the grandmothers,
the givers of genes,

the bearers of dreams—
of paranoia.

JOANNE SELTZER of Schenectady, New York, has authored three chapbooks: *Adirondack Lake Poems* (The Loft Press, 1985), *Suburban Landscape* (M.A.F. Press, 1988) and *Inside Invisible Walls* (Bard Press, 1989). Her poems have been widely published in literary magazines and anthologies, and she has published short fiction, essays, reviews and translations of French poetry.

THE NEW BATHING SUIT
Marguerite Hiken

My grandmother had the morning planned. "Wake up, love," she said to me, climbing out of our shared double bed. She gave me a gentle nudge with her large hand. I slowly opened my eyes and watched her walk around the room, trying to decide which clothes to put on. "Landsakes," she said, "we have a lot to do today."

I crawled out of bed and carelessly slipped into my shoes and brightly speckled dress. I ran a brush through my hair (the usual two strokes), and appeared before my grandmother, ready to receive and partake of her breakfast and the day's plans. I knew she had something interesting in store for us; I could see it in her sparkling eyes. Being the oldest of four sisters, the mother of four children, and provider for twelve grandchildren, she could always think of interesting ways to entertain any number of us.

"First," she said, "we will go downtown and buy me a new bathing suit."

I couldn't believe it—a new bathing suit. I didn't want to spend a glorious summer morning shopping for a bathing suit, especially since mom, as my cousins and I all called our grandmother, had at least two other suits tucked away somewhere in her closet. Why did she need another one?

"Then," she continued, interrupting my disgruntled thoughts, "we have the revival meeting this afternoon."

I looked forward to the afternoon; revivals were fun. Mom belonged to a church; I don't even know the name of it although I had been baptized in it some years before. They dunked me in a barrel of water while chanting mellow and hallow words. All I remember is going under and taking a last long look at the minister's serious, believing face, hoping he didn't really intend to drown me. Mom has been very conscientious concerning my welfare and has had me baptized in five different, deep southern-based churches. I can clearly remember each minister's face as he pushed me under the water. Mom, I guess, felt I was going to need all the help I could get in life, and anyway, she figured the baptisms couldn't hurt. At the revivals someone was always getting baptized, and so I was relieved knowing I'd be passed by this time.

They're sort of fun to go to. The small town we lived in had a county park right outside the city limits where they used to hold the county fairs. The church had pitched a huge, colorful orange and white striped tent on the grass, rented a lot of chairs, set up the speaker's platform, got the barrel out, and everything was ready to go.

But first, we had to spend a few hours getting my grandmother's bathing suit. She's old, you see, and it would take a while to find one that fit her and one that she would like. Her figure was still important to her and I could picture the questions I would have to answer honestly regarding whether this or that color was or was not flattering to her beautiful, wrinkled body.

Sure enough, after the third store I was exhausted, and still no outfit suited her. Our small town only had one more store. I walked into Joannie's Country Wear with fear and trepidation. This was it, I thought, and there on the rack before my blurry eyes, was the perfect swimming suit. It was navy blue and looked as though it had been made in the twenties. It had no waistline, was slightly padded and hung limply.

"Perfect," I uttered.

"Perfect," mom said, and she bought it.

For my patience, she bought me lunch, a great extravagance, because we didn't have much money in those days. Next on our agenda was the revival. Oh, was it going to be hot in that tent! The heat was already up to 105 degrees by noonday, and inside that tent I could picture passing out at 115 degrees. Everyone there would share the sweat and frenzy, with the perspiration moving from body to body, slowly, like a mist of humid ecstasy.

My cousins refused to attend mom's revivals. However, since I was the oldest female cousin, I felt it was my responsibility to keep track of my grandmother's activities.

We arrived on time. I was hot and I knew mom was hot, because she wore her new bathing suit underneath her dark blue nylon dress. After the revival she intended to go swimming, and all through the meeting all I thought about was a beautiful, clear, and light blue swimming pool; I would dive in and the water's coolness and cleanness would make me feel reborn. I would swim under the water looking for strange, mysterious objects on the bottom of the white concrete, and maybe pretend I was a mermaid in the middle of a sparkling, blue-diamond lagoon.

"All rise, sing praises to the Lord. Glory hallelujah," cried the evangelist. "Cleanse your sins, Jesus the Redeemer, bless this child and..." and on and on. People got pretty worked up at these things. I was impressed by mom's reserve and coolness through the entire time. She was obviously a citadel of strength and religion to all those who knew her. I knew I was at my last revival. I wasn't able to let myself go either to God or to the swaying music and I felt like an outsider to a powerful exchange between God and his devout followers. I shouldn't be there if I couldn't get caught up in the emotional aspect of it, although I certainly did wish the best to those who lost themselves in the frenzied ritual. It must be fun, or an emotional release, or at least, some type of communication with higher elements or beings than our limited, circumspect mortal life. I just couldn't keep my mind off that swimming pool.

After the revival, it was late afternoon, and mom and I climbed into the old Ford and headed for the city's public swimming pool. I quickly noticed that she drove the car not toward the crystal blue, but out toward dry, brown fields.

"Mom? Where are we going?" I asked, petrified. I soon relaxed because I realized we were heading to the house of someone who had a beautiful, forty-foot long, twelve-foot deep pool carved out of the backyard of their country estate. But we didn't know anyone who owned an estate, much less anyone who had their own private swimming pool.

Anyway, we were travelling out to where there were no homes at all, only fields of either weeds of crops. "Mom, where are you going?" I cried, watching my crystal clear, blue water evaporate in the hot, late sun. No answer. Mom was miles away from me and I was merely a passenger in a wind alley of hot valley air blowing me around and bullying me in our decrepit blue Ford.

Finally, mom pulled over to a mound of dry dust, parked the car and got out. I couldn't believe it; we were in the middle of nowhere, as nowhere as one could get. Only an old, wrinkled oak tree and an irrigation ditch shared our isolation.

Mom removed her clothes and stood before the brown, murky and turbid water of the irrigation ditch in her new bathing suit. "Mom!" I cried, "You didn't buy that new suit to go swimming here! You wouldn't do that to me, would you? Mom, please, listen to me." I got out of the car and ran to her side to plead my case.

She wasn't listening to me, though, and continued to walk into the ugly ditch. I heard her murmur, "Sweet Jesus," and hold out her hands as she drew the cool, crystal blue water into her arms.

MARGUERITE HIKEN lives and works in San Francisco. She has published many stories and articles in journals, magazines and newspapers and is currently working on a novel. Many of her stories take place in the Central Valley of California.

THE MUSTARD SEED
To Omi

Monika John

From the Mount of Olives in Jerusalem
I brought her a small branch from an olive tree
and a twig of rosemary,
dried between the pages of a book
during several weeks of travel.

When I visited her a few days later
they stood in a vase filled with water
the stems above the waterline still pale dry green
and the parts submerged now brownish.

I asked her why she had put them in water.
She smiled with a little embarrassment
and waving her finger, said: "You will see."

I asked nothing else and felt insensitive
to have disturbed the growth of the mustard seed
and exposed it to the light before germination.

She is eighty-four years young,
and I never again shall wonder,
who taught me to dream.

At age seventeen MONIKA JOHN of Pacific Palisades, California, immigrated to the United States with her sixty-five-year-old grandmother. After graduation from law school, she joined the district attorney's office as a prosecutor. During the past few years she has travelled extensively. MONIKA JOHN credits her grandmother, who raised her from birth, with helping her gain vision and strength.

PHOTO CREDITS
